Thierry PASTOR

The limits of diplomacy

The clash of East-West dialogue

Thierry Pastor: graduate in law and political science, he has been working as a political advisor for about fifteen years. Initially trained in politics, he specialized in the geopolitics of energy and global security. He has worked in several regions of the world, mainly in Eastern Europe and Asia. He is the co-author of several books on the geopolitics of energy, written with university professors, lawyers and economic intelligence specialists. He works in collaboration with several people with various skills: information systems, blockchain technology including cryptocurrencies, NFTs or metaverses. Thanks to this external expertise, these books were born.

From the same author:

In the shadow of Titans, 2022
The dark power of new weapons, 2022
Last chance, 2022

TABLE OF CONTENTS

Foreword

There is strength in numbers. It is from this premise that we decided to aggregate our skills and build our analyses. With different professional backgrounds and life experiences, we concluded that we had to work together because although we do not seem to come from similar worlds, we found many links. Nothing happens by chance. On the one hand, the scientists: engineers, programmers, precursors of the blockchain and fine connoisseurs of cryptocurrencies. On the other, the political advisor, specialist in political analysis, energy geopolitics and global security issues. Two apparently different worlds. And yet, one thing was obvious: our respective skills were complementary.

We noticed that what seems obvious or simple to understand is not so for most people. Few people can code, encrypt and develop computer programs. Few are also able to decipher the interconnections, the ins and outs that allow us to understand events for which most people will only have a limited understanding. Don't be fooled by this misplaced pretentiousness! In truth, we all have access to many things, but are we given the means to understand them? We assume that the answer is no.

Thanks to the Internet, everyone has access to a considerable flow of information. It is still necessary to be able to select, sort and discern those that provide the reader with a true understanding of things. One only must look at all the uncertainties surrounding the Covid-19 health crisis, the mass of information that contradicts itself and for which many grey areas remain. Our job is to try to understand what is going on around us: decipher, understand, and explain. Our objective, in all humility, is to try to shed light on political, economic, historical, technological, or other themes that will allow you to have another vision of the world around you.

Among the themes we will address, you will find blockchain, cryptocurrencies, energy issues, the evolution of international relations and power games, the emergence of green finance or ESG criteria. The list of topics covered is not exhaustive. However, EVERYTHING is linked! We try to highlight the bridges that link these elements that seem to be independent from each other. One should never trust appearances, especially in a world that is so globalized and even more connected due to technological progress.

Our methodology is as follows: all our publications are dated. Some factual or specific elements may seem obsolete. Certainly... but they have the merit of contextualizing the reflection that we develop. The objective is above all to identify trends, those that are likely to continue over time. The world of analysis is not an exact science, even more so when it deals with disciplines as variable and fluctuating as politics or international relations. We can therefore be wrong. On the other hand, we do our best to argue our points. But we can tell you this: the world is constantly changing... and everything is happening at a dizzying pace. Today's truth is not necessarily tomorrow's one. We must therefore live with the times and understand the causes of these changes. It is from this understanding that you will better understand current events and what surrounds you.

Our books compile reflections on different themes, some of which come up repeatedly. In such cases, it means that we give them a high importance. In our view, they are a major factor in the evolution of international relations, technologies and, more generally, in the major trends that are being set up. It is this last point that we are most interested in: we see that things are happening, but we do not fully understand the mechanisms. However, everything is done so that a new vocabulary is disseminated without it being explicitly defined or its inherent stakes being truly understood. This is what we are trying to do. Blockchain, cryptocurrencies, smart cities and other trendy concepts remain relatively nebulous. Yet they fit perfectly into a political, diplomatic, economic, and more globally societal evolution that we are experiencing at a very high speed. The puzzle is large. It is up to everyone to gather the pieces which compose it and to assemble them.

Power, communication, and misunderstanding
April 2022

What is worse than communicating and not being understood? A first answer could be to say that the deliberate attitude is probably worse than the clumsiness. When reading the media, it is not always easy to understand what comes from a poorly controlled communication or, on the contrary, from a deliberate will to communicate in this way. In this global reflection, we will return at length to the Ukrainian crisis. It is a current and revealing example of the evils that we will expose. The overall feeling that emerges is that there is a dialogue of the deaf between Moscow and the Western world. By the Western world, we mean NATO, the European Union (EU) and more generally all the political, economic, and military allies of what constituted the Western bloc during the Cold War. We use this terminology because the Ukrainian crisis is reminiscent in many ways of that dark period of history that agitated the world for four decades after the Second World War. It is not easy to circumscribe by one name all the countries that support Ukraine in its armed opposition to Russia. Indeed, if NATO is generally mentioned by the media, not all EU member states are part of the Atlantic alliance and vice versa. On the other hand, all of them condemn the Russian military intervention in Ukraine during the night of February 23-24, 2022. Although the media communicate abundantly on the subject, the treatment of the information is interesting to analyze because it happens to be incomplete. The information is true but unfortunately incomplete.

The West fears the threats made by Moscow, particularly those concerning the use of nuclear weapons. The Kremlin has indeed made this threat, which has not been made since the Cold War. These are complicated times. Everyone fears the decisions of Russia's absolute master, Vladimir Putin. He gives the impression that he is ready to give the order to commit the irreparable. The world is trembling. It is trembling even more because the plans devised by the Russian head of state are not going according to plan. He intended to engage in Ukraine and to make his power speak, to challenge the Western world to show that his country is one of the great political and military powers of the planet. He has provoked, while he has always claimed to be open to dialogue. The problem is that diplomatic relations between his country and the Western world are complex. One would almost forget certain past episodes that have contributed to this mutual mistrust, often tinged with animosity.

In the West, his detractors say that Vladimir Putin is lying, that he cannot be trusted. In Moscow, the discourse is different: they expect Russia to be treated as an equal, not to be given the impression that a dominant-dominated relationship is felt by Vladimir Putin. Since he has ruled the world's most spacious country, he has had a tense relationship with the West. He could not bear the fall of the USSR. He loves his country and hopes to restore its former glory. However, he who was trained in the Soviet school does not intend to restore the greatness of the USSR but that of the empire of the Tsars. Many analysts and observers are trying to understand his personality. Some fear that the Ukrainian crisis is the materialization of a worrying health that would lend him irrational desires and incompatible with the exercise of power. In short, some say he is crazy, uncontrollable, and dangerous for world security. It is not for us to judge; we will content ourselves with analyzing the facts and understanding the problems associated with this war in Eastern Europe. They are numerous.

In the West, Russia's military action in Ukraine is unanimously condemned. Old Cold War scents are resurfacing. Vladimir Putin favors this climate of anxiety. He provoked it. He is the bad guy. What's more, he is acting in bad faith and would gladly pass himself off as the victim! In Russia, the vision of the Ukrainian crisis is presented differently. In the Western camp, some will say that the Russian media communicate an official voice, the one dictated by the Kremlin. However, since he has been leading Russia, Vladimir Putin has almost always been in a logic of confrontation with the Western world. He has been incessantly intent on seating Russia at the table of the great nations of world politics. There are undoubtedly good reasons for considering him to be animated by bad faith or even more. However, beyond this assessment, the difficult diplomatic relations between Russia and the Western world should be considered with an approach that goes beyond the mere relationship between statesmen. Although politics and diplomacy are the work of men, international relations are not based solely on the feelings or ambitions of everyone. This naturally contributes to animate them, but one should not hide the cultural weight. The corollary is communication and the power of words. Since international relations involve power games, any power struggle necessarily includes a cultural and communication battle. Russia and China are increasingly asserting themselves against the Western world. In substance, there are similarities. In terms of form, there are differences of approach.

Each state actor develops its own understanding of *hard* and *soft power*. [1] For the Chinese and Russian

---

[1] Author's note: hard power and soft power are theories of international relations. They originate from Joseph Nye, an eminent political scientist and author of numerous internationally recognized books and articles. He was Assistant Secretary of Defense for International Security Issues

examples, we can retort that both implement a different approach in their relations with the Western world for many reasons. China's economic power allows it to understand its place on the world stage in a way that differs from Russia, which is less strong economically, but which poses more of a military threat. Thus, China seeks to conquer the world by developing its impressive project to restore the Silk Roads, while Russia prefers to show its muscles to make itself heard in the Arctic zone or in Eastern Europe. Another argument can be the geographical location which contributes to think the power relations differently. China is geographically distant from the Western powers, while Russia shares borders with some of them.

Other explanations can be given, but each State has its own particularities when it comes to manifesting itself on the international scene. Each one has a particular sensitivity that we could call cultural. This implies that not everyone gives the same definition to the same word. In this logic, it appears that words, while sometimes not being a source of resolution of tensions or crises, can contribute to their escalation. In sum, dialogue is one of the major components of international relations. It can be the source of misunderstandings or clumsiness. On the other hand, it can facilitate understanding or resolve misunderstandings. In brief, in a global environment where power relations are omnipresent, it allows messages to be passed on. In this case, the world is changing at a very high speed. Western

---

under President Clinton from 1994 to 1995. He defends the thesis that hard power is characterized by the traditional means of pressure within the political and military power relations. Soft power is based on a more subtle and flexible power of influence. It can be translated into economic or cultural policies. With Robert Keohane, he founded neoliberal institutionalism, a theoretical vision of international relations in which the power of institutions is great in the international system. Joseph Nye is one of the great names in international relations theory and one of the prestigious references of liberal thought.

domination is no longer so overwhelming since Russia and China are challenging its leadership and do not hesitate to openly oppose it, whereas such a situation would never have been envisaged at the end of the Cold War. The world order has evolved because state powers now feel strong enough to thwart Western expectations for domination over hard and soft power.

The Western world, with the United States in the lead, has aroused a lot of antipathy in the world since the attacks of September 2001. These dramatic events had a considerable impact on international relations because the United States of America had just been attacked on its soil. Someone had dared. The ruling authorities immediately decided that such acts could not go unpunished. War was declared on the al-Qaeda organization and materialized in a joint military intervention in Afghanistan. In 2003, it was Saddam Hussein's Iraq's turn to suffer the American wrath for more obscure reasons: the regime was suspected of holding weapons of mass destruction, an argument that turned out to be false. The long military interventions in these lands of Islam resulted in the socio-political destabilization of Iraq and Afghanistan, the rise of terrorism through the emergence of new organizations and the appearance of an anti-American or even anti-Western sentiment that began to spread, particularly in the Islamic world.

Several jurisdictions where Islam is the dominant religion have severely criticized the way the Western world has intervened in Iraq and Afghanistan, but also the discourse of the latter, which is resolutely oriented towards a fierce determination to hunt down terrorist organizations. The way of communicating has often been criticized. The recurrence of certain words or expressions in the Western discourse has led to misunderstandings that have widened the gap of misunderstanding between peoples. While the global discourse constantly hammers home the need to fight against terrorist organizations and authoritarian regimes that transgress human rights, some warn of the risks of amalgamation and misunderstanding. In other words, actors fighting what is denounced by the West have come to express their dismay at being perceived as complacent towards terrorist organizations or as favoring the imposition of authoritarian regimes.

A similar observation can be made in the way the Western world maintains complex relations with Russia. Seen from Europe, the land of the Tsars is perceived as a permanent threat. The outbreak of hostilities in Ukraine was a death knell for Vladimir Putin, who already had little credit in the eyes of the West. He is now described as a threat to world peace and security. He is said to be dangerous and crazy, driven by an unwavering determination to go to the point of no return. However, when we look back, we must recognize that the West bears some responsibility for what has shaped the difficult diplomatic relations with Moscow. We will come back to this: if the military operation launched by Russia is condemnable, we must be careful not to give it all the blame. Several factors have contributed to this unfortunately dramatic context. One obvious factor is the bias of the communication. The war in Ukraine is obviously attributed to the sole Russian will to create chaos in Eastern Europe.

However, in the past, Russia had reacted on many occasions against Western wishes which it disapproved of and which it considered as provocations against it. We could mention the proposals made to Ukraine and Georgia in 2006 to join NATO... Since then, the climate has not ceased to be tense with Moscow but the West, dominated by the United States, must not be absolved of its responsibilities. We will also mention the Minsk Agreement (2014) and Minsk II (2015), which were supposed to lead to the cessation of hostilities between Ukraine and Russia. If the first agreement was never respected, the second was only partially respected by Kiev and Moscow. Here again, the weight of words is fundamental. It is easy to practice a communication policy of denunciation, victimization and even demonization that is effective in attributing the wrong role to an actor while taking care to hide part of the information to deliver a "truth" to public opinion. Dear reader, please understand that in international relations, the origin of many conflicts can be likened to a marital crisis: it is rare that all the blame falls on one and only single actor.

In power games, one weakens one's opponent by putting him down. He is not nice. He is dangerous. Examples are given that tend to confirm these allegations. By dint of hammering this discourse, public opinion acquiesces and ends up assimilating the version delivered. The examples of the fight against Islamic terrorism and the complex relations with Russia are two different cases that show the complexity of the power of communication and the misunderstandings that can be induced by it... or that are desired. As for countries where the population is predominantly Muslim, the Western discourse is insecure. It is clumsy. Thus, by dint of being hammered, it resounds in the ears of its recipients as a form of barely masked accusation. The feeling is as follows: "you suspect us of being the accomplices of terrorists". For Russia, the context is different. It is easy to forget to recall the episodes that contributed to the current Ukrainian crisis. It is the result of a long period of low blows from both sides, the Russian and the Western. Today, the Kremlin is being blamed. The accusations are justified. However, it is still necessary to proceed to a self-criticism and to recognize the wrongs that have contributed to these difficult relations with Russia. In short, some misunderstandings result from clumsiness. Others are deliberate.

An evolving world order

We have already mentioned this theme in another study [2] : the world order has changed considerably since we entered the 21st century. The post-Cold War Western ultra-domination is not so true anymore. This applies to both hard and soft power. The world has changed. States have experienced a meteoric economic rise. Some have since become militarily powerful. Others are more vocal and openly challenge actors that they would never have criticized in this way at the height of Western, and particularly American, domination. The ambitions of some have changed considerably as they feel stronger or are reassured by the fact that others no longer hesitate to challenge or even revolt against the dominant powers. When China promotes its pharaonic Silk Roads infrastructure initiative, everyone understands that it has an economic strike force that only the United States can compete with. When Russia makes claims in the Arctic region, everyone understands that its arguments are serious and intended to embarrass the other countries bordering the region... with the geopolitical consequences that this may entail. When North Korea engages in ballistic launches or nuclear tests, the Western world is outraged but remains desperately powerless in the face of Kim Jong-Un's decisions. This last example is revealing. North Korea is an economic dwarf compared to the United States and its Western allies. The fact that the regime has weapons that are feared by the international community ensures the Kim dynasty's tranquility. Moreover, if Muammar Gaddafi and Saddam Hussein had managed to acquire nuclear military

---

[2] Thierry Pastor, *In the shadow of Titans*, 2022, 208 pp.

power, they would probably never have been overthrown. For this reason, Iran does not intend to give up its nuclear ambitions: the more Tehran manages to maintain this leverage, the more likely the Revolutionary Guards will be to keep the reins of power. Moreover, while the country continues to be subject to numerous economic sanctions aimed at weakening the power of its political and religious leaders, China is trading with Iran, much to the chagrin of the United States. Some European countries had hoped to be able to work with Tehran again, but Washington had made it clear to reckless companies that they would then be exposed to major sanctions... On the other hand, the United States could not say the same thing about China.

Western domination is more than ever challenged. When the events of September 2001 occurred in Uncle Sam's country, the Western world was shocked to discover that it was not impervious to chaos. While the name al-Qaeda quickly became common knowledge, Islamist movements were not in themselves a novelty. Worse, in the case of the organization led by Osama bin Laden, some of its members had once been supported by the United States during the war between Afghanistan and the USSR in the 1980s. These organizations did not suddenly appear on the international scene. Instead, they began to express themselves in an unexpected and offensive way to the Western world and to all those who were then identified as enemies. Many predominantly Christian Western countries, as well as other predominantly Muslim jurisdictions, have been the targets of terrorist attacks. Military interventions in Iraq and Afghanistan have done nothing but create more disorder in the areas concerned and foster the emergence or confirmation of ever more threatening terrorist organizations. Clearly, Western interventions have been a failure. This means that despite economic and military power, no armed intervention guarantees success at the end of the operations. The fact that the West has been bogged down in crises that have lasted longer than expected has undoubtedly contributed to the rise of protests that would probably not have been expressed in this way a few years earlier. The rise in economic, political, and military power of certain state actors also had an impact. Yet, at the end of the Cold War, the American hard and soft powers had never known an equivalent of domination in history. The United States was promised a long period of ultra-domination. A decade later, the situation had already changed considerably.

A post-Cold War context conducive to the eruption of Islamist terrorism

The 20th century has witnessed international turmoil unprecedented in comparison with previous centuries. A combination of factors contributed to wars being more deadly than ever, while a large part of the world was affected by several conflicts or crises. Due to diplomatic and military alliances, colonization, and technological progress, the two world wars were unprecedented in human history. The world was truly on fire during the decade that these two wars lasted. Not a single continent was spared. At the end of the First World War, great empires disappeared. The negotiators of the Treaty of Versailles wanted to make sure that such a human horror would never happen again. Two decades later, a repeat scenario took shape. In the meantime, authoritarian regimes had taken root in several European jurisdictions. The economic crisis of 1929 occurred, and its consequences spread rapidly across Europe. It favored the irresistible rise of Nazism in Germany, which was opposed to the Versailles diktat. In Russia, Lenin, the father of the October Revolution of 1917, died in 1924. Stalin succeeded him and ruled the USSR with an iron fist until 1953. In Italy, Mussolini's fascism ruled the country for two decades. In Western Europe, the

United Kingdom encountered several internal political crises. This resulted in a succession of Prime Ministers. While some managed to hold their position for several years, others saw their governmental action limited to a few weeks or months. In France, the Third Republic showed signs of running out of steam: governments were often disavowed by Parliament. Between 1920 and the establishment of the Vichy regime in July 1940, there were no less than forty-five changes in the presidency of the Council of Ministers. Twelve governments lasted less than a month (Raymond Poincaré twice managed to lead a government for two years... he was the only one to achieve such a feat)! This contributed to an instability of governance because of the constant changes of the leading teams. Similarly, in the case of the United Kingdom and France, these two colonial powers also had to deal with protest movements that were beginning to emerge in several colonies.

Adolf Hitler's expansionist ambitions worried his interlocutors, who did their best to avoid a new war. Despite French and British diplomatic efforts, Europe was once again in flames in 1939. If the armies of the Reich seemed to easily conquer the West and the East, the opening of several fronts meant that the war spread over an immense geographical area. Through the interplay of alliances and provocations, many countries found themselves involved in this world war, which undoubtedly reached the height of ignominy. Several tens of millions of people died. After six years of bitter fighting, Nazi Germany and its Japanese ally surrendered. The world hoped to learn from this terrible war and never face such a situation again. The world barely had time to breathe before the Cold War began. With it, an ideological opposition was going to animate the world and divide it into two great groups: the East and the West. Two state powers were to oppose each other: the United States and the USSR. Similarly, another threat was to symbolize this exacerbated rivalry: nuclear weapons.

In the meantime, the world was also evolving at great speed. Decolonization had begun, but it included tragic episodes with the outbreak of wars of independence. Asia and Africa experienced numerous crises, some of which are still ongoing, such as the rivalry between India and Pakistan. Many new independent states were born. For some, this was done in pain. France had to manage the Indochina war which later became the Vietnam war with the American intervention. There was also the Algerian war of independence. In the meantime, a conflict was raging in the Far East in the Korean peninsula since 1950 (despite the cease-fire of July 1953). In China, Mao Zedong proclaimed the People's Republic in October 1949, a communist regime that he ruled firmly until his death in 1976. In the 1960s, as the Cold War intensified, several countries with wealth that they now intended to exploit for their own benefit joined forces in a cartel: the OPEC was born. This organization would gradually gain importance in the international landscape as black gold gained increasing influence in the world economy and international relations. These are just a few examples to show the turmoil that was shaking the post- World War for several decades.

The second half of the 20th century was therefore tumultuous. In Western Europe, the time for reconstruction had come after the war. It was accompanied by a clear desire for peace. The 1950s witnessed the first stages of what would become European construction, notably through the creation of the European Coal and Steel Community and the European Atomic Energy Community. The idea was to bring together the enemies of yesteryear, France, and Germany in the first place, within inter-state organizations. It was not easy to bring together these two countries that had been at odds in three wars in just seven decades. The challenge was daring but successful. The European Economic Community was created in 1957 and brought together France, Germany, Italy and the three Benelux countries. This supranational organization expanded little by little until it became a political and economic union in 1992: the EU. The famous Maastricht Treaty of 1992 came after several major events that animated the preceding years. There was the fall of the Berlin Wall in 1989. The first Gulf War broke out in 1990. The end of the USSR was finally decided in 1991. In other words, in two years, the world witnessed the end of the Cold War and the confirmation of a new world order. The East-West rivalry came to an end, while the triumph of the West was affirmed more than ever, notably through the invasion of Kuwait by Saddam Hussein's Iraq. The intervention of a coalition force led by the United States symbolized the new reorganization of the world, which then witnessed the confirmation of an unequalled power in terms of hard and soft power: that of the United States of America. American domination was such that it was difficult to imagine that it could be challenged by anyone. No one had the political, economic, military, technological or cultural capacity to compete with it.

However, a few warning signs were to remind us that power games are evolving and that nothing is ever definitively acquired in international relations. In the 1990s, the United States was the target of several terrorist attacks. In February 1993, a car bomb hit the World Trade Centre in New York. It killed six people and injured over a thousand. In August 1998, bombings targeted the U.S. embassies in Nairobi, Kenya, and Dar es Salaam, Tanzania. Two hundred and twenty-four people were killed and over four thousand injured. In October 2000, the American destroyer USS Cole was the target of a suicide attack in Aden, Yemen.

Seventeen American soldiers lost their lives. In the meantime, a name had begun to circulate among Western intelligence agencies: al-Qaeda. On September 11, 2001, the world was gripped by fear with the hijacking of several airliners in the United States and the attacks that forever marked the beginning of the third millennium. On that day, the world's leading economic power suffered the most severe attack on its territory since Pearl Harbor in December 1941. The latter was ordered by Japan and precipitated the entry of the United States into the Second World War. However, the events of 9/11 were not the work of a state but of an international terrorist organization with multiple ramifications. President George W. Bush immediately ordered the tracking down of the perpetrators of these attacks. A war was to be declared against an enemy that was not a state.

Reducing power differentials and challenging Western power dominance

There was a before and after September 11, 2001. There are dates that deeply mark history, and this is one of them. The attacks were not the cause of a revolution in the world order. If these events are by their nature of extreme brutality, the world order has evolved little by little. However, 9/11 signaled a new order: a new enemy had emerged. Al-Qaeda not only claimed responsibility for the attacks, but also announced its intention to continue its fight against those actors who had been identified as enemies. For the United States, a new kind of war was about to begin because, unlike a conventional army, the enemy could now be anyone. In other words, while the military intervention in Afghanistan was aimed at fighting the Taliban and al-Qaeda, not all members of this organization lived in Central Asia. Many of the sympathizers and activists were based in the West.

The beginning of the 21st century was also marked by the rise in political, economic, and military power of several states that would gradually assert themselves on the international scene. In 2000, a man took over the reins of Russia at the end of the Yeltsin era: Vladimir Putin. He quickly set the rules of the game and showed a formidable and feared intransigence towards anyone who stood in his way. He put up a fierce fight against the terrorist organizations that carried out attacks in Russia. As for the business community, the oligarchs understood that they could develop their business as they wished, but they were ordered not to interfere in the political affairs of the country. A new authority had been established in Russia, and the prices of many commodities, starting with hydrocarbons, allowed the country to enjoy an economic boom that almost made people forget the economic disaster caused by the collapse of the USSR a decade earlier. The Russian economic recovery was spectacular. As for the country's national ambitions, they were soon to be exposed: Vladimir Putin clearly stated his intention to make his country a major power in the world political arena. He sent a message to the West that it should talk to Russia as equals. Very quickly, the issues of contention became apparent. The diplomatic gap between Moscow and the Western alliance only grew with time.

Jiang Zemin, Hu Jintao, Xi Jinping. These are the names of the three political leaders who have steered China's political and economic destiny since the 1990s. Since the 1960s, the country has enjoyed high rates of economic growth. In the best years, it exceeded 20%. This was while the national economy was lagging far behind the dynamism of the world's most advanced economies. However, although growth rates gradually declined, they have always remained dynamic. Moreover, in the 2000s, economic analysts did not imagine that China could continue its economic development marked by such high growth rates (above 5% at least and sometimes close to 10%). The Chinese giant has not made any noise. It has continued its economic development step by step until it has become a key player in the world economy. China experienced a meteoric rise to power in the 2000s. It organized the Summer Olympic Games in Beijing in 2008. They were the most expensive in history. It was able to free itself from external pressure when it was criticized for its policy towards Tibet. Later, it displayed the same imperviousness to external pressure regarding Xinjiang and Hong Kong. The arrival in power of Xi Jinping brought the country into another dimension with the promotion of the ambitious initiative to restore the Silk Roads. The budget allocated (one thousand billion dollars) is unique for such an infrastructure project. Above all, Beijing is demonstrating its extraordinary ambitions to optimize its commercial interests on several continents. Finally, China has also made immense progress in the technological field. It has communicated extensively on its space projects. It has become a reference for new technologies. It is devoting a growing budget to its defense. Only the United States devotes more money than it does to this sensitive sector. As for its diplomacy, it cares little for Western warnings. It does not fear them. Who could, for example, impose on China not to trade with Iran?

The balance of power is constantly changing in international relations. In view of the war in Ukraine, the European powers have decided to spend more on their defense. Russia acted on the night of 23 to 24 February 2022. If everyone agreed to give credence to the hypothesis of a Russian offensive, the act revealed above all the unpreparedness of several European powers, which confessed that they were not ready to engage in an armed conflict. This offensive was a reminder that war is an immutable component of international relations. Despite all that the international community has been able to put in place to prevent the risks of conflict, there are still problems for which diplomacy is unfortunately powerless or ineffective. However, we should not underestimate the power of diplomacy, as it has repeatedly allowed crises to be resolved through dialogue. Although we defend the postulate that the reason of the strongest always prevails, this was all the truer at the height of American domination. The latter is obviously no longer as striking as it once was. When it was still possible to obtain satisfaction with the use of threats, sometimes force, or simply by imposing one's will through communications in which the imperative tone dominated, the situation has changed due to the reduction of power gaps with competing actors. While it is important to be firm, it is equally important to adapt communication to the contemporary reality of international relations.

Weight of words and misinterpretations

Being a diplomat is not an easy job. Communicating is an art. In antiquity, Aristotle had long wondered about the art of rhetoric. He had articulated it around three main ideas: *ethos, logos,* and *pathos.* The *ethos* focuses on the speaker, his personality and everything that allows him to be convincing. The *logos* is the argumentative part of the communication. As for *pathos,* it refers to the emotional part of the speech. It is what makes the other person aware. Aristotle is obviously not the only thinker to have considered the theme of rhetoric; on the other hand, his reflection dates from the fourth century before our era and it remains perfectly adapted to the communication we know because any form of communication rests on a report of seduction. If the magic does not work, the seduction operation will be a failure. This is the difficulty that falls to the diplomat. He must seduce his interlocutors who will in turn have arguments to put forward. Similarly, he must also take into consideration the cultural and other differences of his alter egos: diplomacy refers to the ideas developed by Aristotle but induces a less apparent dimension: balance. It is indeed a balance because diplomacy triumphs when the parties involved manage to agree peacefully on an opposition, a disagreement or even a crisis. This is a sign that the interventions of diplomats have paid off. The arguments have been convincing. Reason has prevailed. However, it also means that the actors managed to communicate without making mistakes. In other words, everyone took care to consider the other despite their differences. Sometimes these differences are not apparent. For example, the diplomat must make sure that the words he uses will be perfectly understood by his interlocutors. Communicating therefore means making sure that the other person understands the meaning of what is being said. But this is never easy.

In his realistic vision of international relations, Raymond Aron saw two characters as those who best embodied or symbolized them: the soldier and the diplomat. Although this thesis has been criticized for obscuring other actors (intelligence agents, people in charge of disseminating propaganda, etc.), it does have the merit of presenting a synthetic vision of the way the world works. Of course, it is indeed reductive to limit international relations to diplomacy and war, since there are other means of action and communication, but let us grant the diplomat and the soldier the roles of the most visible actors on the international scene in the event of a political crisis involving several countries. The first is the communicator, the one who seeks solutions that aim to resolve problems to avoid the option of armed conflict. The second embodies the failure of diplomacy. By failure, we must understand that diplomacy does not resolve all disagreements. Misunderstandings may remain. Similarly, the failure of dialogue may be due to the deliberate desire of one or more of the parties involved to engage in armed conflict.

Communicating remains a complicated exercise in style because one must put forward arguments that are admissible and ultimately convincing. It is necessary to ensure that the words used are assimilated in the same way by all. It is therefore necessary to be concerned with the perception that an interlocutor will have of certain words in each cultural and political reality. Thus, using the word "democracy" at all times in a discussion with representatives of an authoritarian regime is risky if it is a deliberate attempt to communicate in this way and awkward if it is not intentional. Thus, communication incorporates the frequency of words used as well as an overall tone. This refers to Aristotle's *pathos*: the content of a speech as well as its tone will have an impact on its recipients. Thus, when the Western world experienced a major wave of terrorist attacks in the 2000s claimed by al-Qaeda, it was extremely difficult for the targeted countries to show an unwavering determination to fight against terrorist organizations and to hammer home a discourse in which the recipient ended up not really discerning the real objective of the message. Clearly, as we have already mentioned, countries with an Islamic culture ended up being indignant about the Western discourse because they felt that Westerners were assimilating them. While the discourse was intended to be categorical about the will to fight terrorist organizations, the repetition of the desire to fight religious extremism and the tone of the discourse caused public authorities to raise the following question: do you think we are complicit and complacent towards terrorist organizations?

We are convinced that the Western world has never sought to make the public authorities of jurisdictions of Islamic culture feel targeted by reproaches or even implied accusations. Indeed, a large majority of them actively fight terrorist organizations. Some of them have suffered murderous attacks. However, too frequently recurring remarks give them the impression of being suspected of leniency or even complicity when this was not the goal of the Western world. Therefore, dialogue is not just a series of words and phrases. It is imperative to know how the other will receive and assimilate them, just as it is essential to care about the way of communicating. Every detail is important because everything is subject to misinterpretation or misunderstanding that can be a source of discord. In other words, although there was no initial bad intention, the cure may turn out to be worse than the disease. We feel that this is all the truer in a global environment where the once ultra-dominant actors on the international scene are seeing competition intensify in terms of both hard and soft power. Let our analysis not be misinterpreted! We are not advising Western powers to bow to the rise of competing actors that challenge their political, economic, military, technological or cultural dominance. No. We are advising them to adapt their discourse to the reality of the evolution of international relations. Those who wish to remain powerful in a global environment where competition is intensifying will not be able to assuage their wishes by opting for the systematic imposition of force. It is therefore necessary to be firm but also to be subtle. After all, was it not Machiavelli who, in the 16th century, advised the Prince to use the cunning of the fox and the strength of the lion to govern effectively? [3]

Conclusion

The world has changed considerably since the year 2000. This is a certainty. The reality of international relations in the 1990s has been swept away by several factors that we have tried to highlight. The balance of power

---

[3] Niccoló Machiavelli, *The Prince*, 1513 but first published in 1532

is changing at a very high speed. Similarly, the 2010 decade has brought confirmation: the Western world is experiencing internal socio-political crises that tend to give pride of place to populist or demagogic policies. This is a clear sign that something is wrong. Although he was elected on the Republican Party ticket, Donald Trump was a UFO on the international political scene. With little respect for protocol, he is the cause of a cooling of relations with traditional US allies. We can also mention the election of Jair Bolsonaro, a far-right candidate, in Brazil. We can mention the popularity of far-right political actors in Europe: Marine Le Pen in France, who managed to reach the second round of the French presidential elections of 2017 and 2022, Matteo Salvini in Italy, who was a minister under the Conte government but who is the head of a political party sometimes presented as the most popular in Italy, or Sebastian Kurz in Austria, who even served as Chancellor of his country.

In the West, the moderate parties traditionally in power are increasingly challenged by voters, who are now shifting their votes to the extremes. As for the other states that seriously compete with Western leadership, they are led by strongmen who impose their authority on everyone in their country. There are thus important differences in political regimes and methods of governance: the communication of an authoritarian leader generally differs from that of a more moderate leader with fewer prerogatives of public power in his hands. In other words, this is evident in the communication between these different types of leaders, especially when the balance of power tends to be reduced among the world's major political, economic, and military powers. This probably makes dialogue more complicated. The art of communication is even more formidable.

It is only a hypothesis, but all these elements may be part of the explanation for the difficult diplomatic relations that Russia has had with the Western world since the advent of Vladimir Putin. We will never know if the war between Russia and Ukraine was avoidable. Perhaps nothing would have prevented Vladimir Putin from wanting to engage in a Russian military intervention with his neighbor, that despite diplomatic efforts, he intended to engage in combat. Perhaps he was ready for a sincere dialogue, as he has often said, to avoid a war. It is said that the Russians and the West could not find a common ground that would suit everyone (including Ukraine). Perhaps. However, we still believe that diplomatic efforts could have paid off and mitigated the Russian-Ukrainian crisis. There were undoubtedly communication errors made. There was undoubtedly bad faith which destroyed the chances of a diplomatic outcome. There was certainly a problem of dialogue between the parties involved.

After two months of fighting between the Russian and Ukrainian armed forces, and despite diplomatic discussions in Turkey to find common ground to end the hostilities, Russia did not expect to encounter so many difficulties with its opponent. Civilian and military casualties are numerous. In the West, it is believed that President Putin has overestimated his military capabilities. In Russia, the popularity of the latter continues to grow while the intervention in Ukraine was supposed to be a matter of a few days.

Russia has carried out its threats. This military intervention has shocked the Western world. We wonder. If Ukraine plays the bad role of the country that is attacked and must defend itself, the Russian offensive is a message to the Western world beyond the one that was sent to Kiev. In short, how should we understand Russia-Western relations? Are they the result of a real problem of mutual understanding or are they based on a real intention not to understand each other? We will see throughout this book that there are undoubtedly real misunderstandings on both sides. However, there are also arguments in favor of a deliberate desire to have fought on the ground. Until now, the Atlantic alliance has never considered fighting against the Russian armed forces. It supports Ukraine with funds and logistics, but no NATO armed forces are fighting Russia. Vladimir Putin intentionally started the hostilities in Ukraine. He is defying the entire Western world. War is a way for him to communicate. The Western alliance does not intend to communicate in this way unless it has no choice but to engage in an armed struggle. The West thinks that Vladimir Putin has overestimated his strengths. He seems sure of what he is doing and communicates in this sense. He wants to show the Western world that the balance of power has changed on the international scene. This is his vision. As far as communication is concerned, we believe that it must be adapted to the reality of international relations in terms of the balance of power. This applies to everyone if the objective is to avoid wars.

Meanwhile, Kazakhstan is on the verge of a precipice...
January 2022

In the largest country in Central Asia, the transition to the new year was accompanied by unrest that quickly took on an unexpected dimension. The latter spread as far as Almaty, the former capital and main economic hub of the country. The liberalization of liquefied petroleum gas (LPG) prices was the source of this popular discontent, as they suddenly doubled on January 1. In a country where most of the population uses LPG, this decision was the one too that could not be accepted anymore, the one that would provoke a massive reaction. The people took to the streets in protest, seeing their low purchasing power severely impacted. These reactions were quickly repressed. The first deaths came to mark this episode of popular discontent. Everything started from several coastal cities of the Caspian Sea. Very quickly, the movement crossed the country and spread to Almaty where the popular protest took on the appearance of an insurrection. The reaction of the national authorities was radical: the police were ordered to shoot at the crowd. This decision shocked both Kazakhstan and the international community, and some countries supported the decision of President Kassym-Jomart Tokayev. Meanwhile, the government resigned.

This is how the events were presented in the West. Nevertheless, it had to be admitted that little information came from Kazakhstan. However, it was learned that the head of the intelligence services, former Prime Minister Karim Massimov, had been arrested. Similarly, President Tokayev had just done the unthinkable by ousting his predecessor Nursultan Nazarbayev from the presidency of the Security Council, a body that had allowed the former President to retain a great deal of influence in the political life of his country since his official retirement in 2019. In short, social tensions are the tree that hides the forest. The real issues are to be found elsewhere: we are witnessing a coup d'état against a backdrop of social chaos. A state of emergency has since been declared. As for the population, it no longer has access to the Internet. For several days, we have not had any contact with friends living in the country. It seems that the time when President Tokayev referred to Nursultan Nazarbayev when talking about the economic progress made by Kazakhstan under his leadership is over. It was under his aegis that the capital Astana was renamed in 2019 to Nur-Sultan. He now intends to show that the Nazarbayev page is closing and that a new chapter in national history is being written. However, this initiative is extremely risky. Yet, once again, the information conveyed in the West does not accurately reflect the reality. The reality is indeed more complex. As for President Tokayev's decisions, they need to be commented on. Some light is needed.

This beginning of the year is tragic in many ways. Firstly, we think of all those people who lost their lives in these scuffles that were unfortunately not unexpected. Secondly, we will try to explain why this social and political chaos occurred later than we could have imagined. Finally, how can we fail to provide some explanations for the Western reactions which have mainly revolved around the Russian intervention in Kazakhstan, at the request of President Tokayev? Unfortunately, once again, the Western world has opinions that are not adapted to the reality of the situation. Moreover, this is an observation that we have been making for too many years. The reactions of Brussels, Paris or Berlin are inappropriate to what Kazakhstan is going through. It is legitimate that these capitals are concerned about a situation that is developing dangerously. The problem is that the interpretation of events is far from reality. It is regrettable to note that accusatory communication is so easy to use when it would be more appropriate to refrain from making judgments about societies and peoples whose habits and customs we do not know, let alone their history. So why this strong reaction on our part? The reason is simple: one of us knows this country well and used to live there. But the observation remains the same: the Western world does not know Central Asia. The Western world does not know this region of the world, which has a rich history. The Western world does not know the steppe and its great nomadic peoples who knew the Mongolian empire, that of the Tsar and then the Soviet era before moving towards independence after the Cold War. These lands rich in natural resources are coveted by various foreign powers. Kazakhstan is by far the world's largest producer of uranium. This Central Asian country has numerous mining resources. Wedged between Russia, China, and the other former Soviet republics of Central Asia, it has been struggling for three decades not to fall under the yoke of a foreign power. These beautiful people are proud, and they have reason to be so. And woe betide anyone who does not show sufficient respect for this great land of the steppe! Former French President François Hollande can testify to this. In December 2014, the unfortunate man was forced to pose in traditional clothes and an invasive shapka alongside his Kazakhstani counterpart [4] with an impeccable smile in his suit and tie, during a state visit. A photo quickly circulated in the media and embarrassed the Elysée for some time. This occurred at a time when bilateral relations between France and Kazakhstan were not at their best, which had an impact on

---

[4] Author's note: Kazakhstani is not to be confused with Kazakh. Kazakhstani is the person who holds the citizenship of the country. Kazakh is a person who belongs to the Kazakh ethnic group which is dominant in the country.

French foreign trade with the main political and economic power in Central Asia.

In the West, we always make the same mistake: criticizing without knowing. The current events that are troubling the country are regrettable and dramatic. They are the consequence of different causes. We hope that everything will return to normal as soon as possible and that no more blood will be shed in the streets. The Republic Square in Almaty was taken over by the demonstrators who shouted their anger and demanded that the former ruling elites leave power. However, in the West, there was no mention of some of the agitators who were "invited" to come and participate in the disorder. This is precisely what led to the arrest of the head of the intelligence services on charges of "high treason". The tumultuous events in Almaty were not related to the problem of rising gas prices on January 1. The chaos in the former capital occurred precisely at the intersection of the main streets, Satpayeva and Zheltoqsan (December in Kazakh language), where there is a large statue commemorating the tragic events of December 1986, when a student revolt was put down in blood on the orders of the Kremlin and Mikhail Gorbachev. History repeats itself with the difference that Kazakhstan has since become an independent and sovereign state... but that it is the object of many geopolitical interests. We will try to decipher them. As for the major European capitals which see in the Russian military intervention a sort of déjà vu scenario regarding Ukraine, the cases are fundamentally different. Russia intervened at the request of President Tokayev within the framework of an international agreement that links Moscow to Nur-Sultan and other former Soviet capitals. As for President Putin, such a military intervention is also an opportunity to regain some influence in a country where Chinese economic power has eclipsed Moscow's interests for the past fifteen years. The great game is being set up before our eyes.

Kazakhstan, strategic crossroads, and hub of Central Asia
        Country located in the heart of Central Asia, it is part of this region poorly known to the Western world. However, as discreet as it may be on the international scene, it is the ninth largest country in terms of surface area, which is slightly more than two million seven hundred thousand square kilometers, and a national population of less than nineteen million individuals. Its population density is among the lowest in the world. Kazakhstan is essentially a desert country, and its main cities are usually several hundred kilometers away. However, the country is rich in natural resources. Known for its oil and gas deposits, in 2021 it was the world's thirteenth largest producer of crude oil. Its daily production was close to one million six hundred thousand barrels. [5] To give an idea, its production is slightly lower than that of Norway and Mexico, but higher than that of Nigeria and Angola. It also has a dynamic iron ore mining sector with abundant reserves of manganese, iron, and chromium, for which Kazakhstan is one of the world's ten largest holders. It is also one of the world's ten largest producers of coal and, as mentioned in the introduction, it is by far the world's largest producer of uranium. Finally, it should be noted that all these natural resources have the immense advantage of being easily accessible and exploitable, as is the case with oil from the Arabian Peninsula. In short, this country essentially composed of steppe has been blessed by the gods! For the reasons mentioned above, it is indeed the main political and economic powerhouse of the region, except that it has the particularity of sharing common borders with Russia and China. A former Soviet republic, Kazakhstan has been an

---

[5]   https://fr.tradingeconomics.com/country-list/crude-oil-production, accessed February 1, 2022

independent and sovereign state since 1991. Nursultan Nazarbayev was its first and only President until his withdrawal in 2019. In the West, few had heard of this country, Central Asia was mostly perceived to be composed of authoritarian systems driven by large families who monopolized the control of political power while defending huge economic interests that were to establish their wealth. The years of Nazarbayev's rule were indeed marked by such abuses, which allowed several families to enrich themselves considerably. In the years 2000 and 2010, this led to the freezing in Europe of many bank assets held by Kazakh personalities or institutions. Similarly, the regime has been criticized for managing social life too strictly, out of step with the democratic values advocated by the Western world, as during the dramatic events that took place in the city of Zhanaozen in 2011, referring to a strike of oil workers that ended with severe police repression. This event marked the spirits in Europe. It was condemned by the Council of Europe, an institutional organization that defends human rights, of which Kazakhstan is a member.

On the other hand, it was precisely during the Nazarbayev presidency that the country experienced dynamic economic growth thanks to the exploitation of natural resources. Thus, in the 1990s, the national capital was moved to the Northern center of the country. Indeed, President Nazarbayev considered that the city of Almaty was too far away because it was geographically close to the Kyrgyz border and specially to neighboring China. It was therefore decided to relocate the decision-making center to the middle of the steppe, to Astana. Contrary to popular belief, the national authorities did not have the fantasy of creating a new city in the middle of the desert. At the current location of the capital, there was a small town that underwent a huge construction site to become this ultra-modern city that some describe as the Dubai of Central

Asia. The administrative center of the country has left Almaty but the city of apples [6] has remained the main national economic lung.

Nursultan Nazarbayev did not deviate from the rule of the political leader wishing to leave his mark on space and time. He has indeed built Astana, but it should not be seen as a capricious wish to transfer a new capital to the desert steppe: this decision was the result of a mature reflection. It was wise to provide the country with a center of power that is more central regarding the national geography. On the other hand, he was a great state manager because beyond the dynamic economic development of Kazakhstan, he was the artisan of a subtle diplomatic policy for which he admirably knew how to defend the national interests. In view of the country's natural wealth and geographical position, it was necessary to show great capacities of governance to know how to satisfy the interests of many foreign powers without this becoming a threat to the stability of the regime. It was not easy to lead a country coveted for its natural resources while Russia, China, the United States, the European Union (EU) and even India wanted to defend different interests, some of which being naturally antagonistic. The former President was able to maneuver skillfully within these international interests and promote Kazakhstan. Thus, in December 2012, he announced the creation of the *Kazakhstan 2050 Strategy* project. [7] The announced objective was to make this Central Asian republic an economic power that should be among the thirty most successful on the planet. To achieve this, Nursultan Nazarbayev focused on the promotion of new sectors of activity such as tourism and sustainable

---

[6] Author's note: this is the meaning of Almaty in Kazakh language

[7] https://kazakhstan2050.com/, accessed January 31, 2022 Author's note: this is a program of economic development and goals to be achieved by 2050.

development. His ambition has always been to make his country attractive while not falling under the yoke of foreign influence. From this point of view, he was the statesman who knew how to make his country known and recognized on the international scene. However, there was no guarantee that he could modernize Kazakhstan in this way.

The difficult legacy of the Soviet era

The end of the Cold War had a terrible impact on the Soviet Union as it led to its breakup. The Soviet model of governance had reached its limits. Despite Mikhail Gorbachev's policies of reconstruction (*perestroika*) and transparency (*glasnost*), they came too late. The situation was irreversible. The great USSR could no longer hide its economic and social difficulties. The colossus was standing on feet of clay. It would not be long before it collapsed. Some signs had already alerted the Western world, notably the poor crisis management by the Soviet authorities following the Chernobyl nuclear disaster in April 1986. Similarly, the country, which was still relying on oil sales, suffered a severe blow when OPEC flooded the world oil market (this operation was initially the result of an agreement between the United States and Saudi Arabia, with the Wahhabi kingdom then succeeding in convincing the other members of the cartel to increase their oil production), which resulted in a sharp drop in the price of black gold. The economic damage was considerable. In July 1986, a barrel of oil was traded at around $10. The Soviet economy was severely impacted a few weeks after the Chernobyl disaster... Finally, internally, everything went from bad to worse. Some peoples were clearly opposed to the Soviet spirit and asked to emancipate themselves from Moscow. This heavy context only announced the future wars of independence that would mark the effective end of the USSR.

In the West, it is often forgotten that the newly independent and sovereign states created after the break-up of the USSR did not solve their social problems when they left the Soviet ship. Almost all of them had great difficulties in building a national spirit, perhaps except for the Baltic States or Belarus.

The former Soviet Caucasian and Central Asian republics were subjected to Stalinist policies of population displacement. The former absolute master of the Kremlin opted in his time for the policy of "divide and conquer". He based his thinking on an obsession: to ensure that no region is exposed to the risk of local destabilization emerging from a dominant ethnic group. Therefore, nowadays there are still so many problems of ethnic cohabitation in several countries of the former USSR. Central Asia is no exception to this rule. In Kazakhstan, many ethnic groups live together. They are more than one hundred. If the Kazakh ethnic group is dominant and majority, Russians, Tatars, Uzbeks, Kirghiz, Tajiks, Germans, Uyghurs, or Koreans are part of the numerous ethnic groups which compose Kazakhstan. Between some of them, relations are sometimes difficult. Thus, diplomatic relations between Kazakhstan and Uzbekistan are complex and sometimes lead to the closure of the borders between the two countries. This was undoubtedly another of Nursultan Nazarbayev's great achievements: he was able to maintain socio-political stability throughout the country. However, this meant that the population had to be subjected to strict rules. To avoid any form of uncontrollable disorder, he imposed order. In the eyes of the Western world, he will undoubtedly retain the image of a despot. However, in his defense, he had to deal with a complex regional geopolitical reality (regarding the economic and strategic interests of various foreign powers) while the country wanted to embark on an economic modernization that was made difficult by the poor cohabitation of ethnic groups.

An economic emergence achieved through a clever diplomatic balancing act

An iron hand in a velvet glove. The cunning of the fox and the strength of the lion. Both correspond to Nazarbayev's governance for almost three decades. He was a skilled and remarkable negotiator on the international stage. He was also the man who imposed authority in Kazakhstan. Above all, he was the leader who set his country on the path of economic modernization. The first years of governance were complicated but linked to the collapse of the USSR and the promotion of the national economies of the newly created states which was then to be established. According to the World Bank, Kazakhstan has had good economic growth rates since 1999. In the best years they were between 8 and 10%. This rate reached 13.5% in 2001.[8] The economic upturn was partly due to higher oil and gas prices and increased production capacity in the mining sector. Kazakhstan increased export volumes, while internally it focused on developing its financial sector and boosting other industries such as real estate construction. The years 2008 and 2009 were more challenging due to the global financial crisis, but the decade of 2010, except for 2015 and 2016, saw annual GDP growth rates above 4%. [9] This economic performance was made possible by the country's abundant natural resources. However, they were achieved in a complex geopolitical context.

When one has so many natural resources, one inevitably attracts the covetousness of those who seek to

---

[8] *« Croissance du PIB (% annuel) - Kazakhstan »*, donnees.banquemondiale.org, accessed January 31, 2022
[9] *Ibid.*

buy or even exploit them. After the break-up of the USSR, Russia kept privileged links with Kazakhstan. The context at that time was as follows: Astana was under construction; Moscow was being rebuilt and Beijing was beginning to see its national economy emerge. As for the Americans and the Europeans, they were already there! Several large Western oil and gas companies are major shareholders in the consortia that operate the Tengiz, Karachaganak and Kashagan fields. For the first two mentioned, the discoveries were made while Kazakhstan was still part of the USSR. When the country became independent, exploitation companies were created, and this is how the big Western companies had the possibility to access the local natural wealth. The idea was twofold: to work with foreign partners who had the technology and financial means to develop the exploitation of the deposits. On the other hand, it was also a way to establish links with the Western world and to guard against too much Russian political influence while the latter was trying to recover and digest the disappearance of the USSR. However, Russia quickly regained its former glory. A decade was enough to turn it into a state power that counted in the international community, especially in the 2000s when it benefited from the rise in oil prices. However, Russia's influence in Central Asia was to be thwarted by the economic rise of China, which took place at the same time. Beijing's priority was to secure its oil and natural gas supplies and it detected a desire in the oil-producing Central Asian republics to diversify their strategic partnerships with foreign powers. Chinese investments changed the situation in Central Asia. Moreover, new pipeline routes were created, to the detriment of Russia, since the countries of the region remained dependent on the existing pipeline networks, which systematically led back to Russia. Thus, Kazakhstan, Uzbekistan and Turkmenistan were not averse to the opportunity to create new oil and gas pipeline networks that would not transit through Russia.

Chinese investments in Central Asia intensified with the promotion of President Xi Jinping's giant project to restore the Silk Roads. [10] However, President Nazarbayev was careful not to become dependent on China, whose ambitions seemed unlimited. It was therefore important for him to maintain good diplomatic relations with Russia and to do the same with his Western partners. It is in this sense that Nazarbayev's governance was remarkable because the exercise of style was extremely difficult in view of the international stakes debated by various foreign powers. He knew how to manage the susceptibilities of all sides. It means that he managed to satisfy his strategic partners while boosting the economic appeal of his country and contributing to its modernization.

The major problem that would arise regarding the omnipotence of the presidential clan would be the political succession on the day Nursultan Nazarbayev left power. Indeed, although he imposed an authoritarian regime, he was a master at managing his country while showing great charisma. He was able to impose authority, but he had to plan his succession and ensure that it was not chaotic. After almost three decades in power and considering that the national population is young, most Kazakhs have only known him as head of state. However, he was the one who allowed Kazakhstan to make a name for itself in the international community. For any successor, it was necessary to consider the aura of the character and to take the measure of the work accomplished on the international scene while not hiding the internal social difficulties. When

---

[10] See Thierry Pastor, *The dark power of new weapons*, 2022, 233 pp.

he resigned from the presidency of the Republic in 2019, a question arose: what would happen in Kazakhstan?

A political chaos unfortunately predictable

It is always risky to succeed a man who has held the reins of power for so long in a country. When Kassym-Jomart Tokayev took over, that is when we feared for Kazakhstan. However, nothing bad happened, as if the succession had been carefully orchestrated. It must be admitted that the new interim President was no stranger to the people of Kazakhstan as he had previously been the country's Foreign Minister, Prime Minister, Director General of the United Nations Office in Geneva and twice President of the Senate. In other words, his political experience spoke positively for him, and he had made a name for himself on the international scene. In short, with such a profile, it was logical that Kassym-Jomart Tokayev succeeded Nursultan Nazarbayev, to whom he was also very close. This was even more so because the national Constitution provided that in the event of a power vacuum, the interim was ensured by the President of the Senate. At that time, Kassym-Jomart Tokayev was in charge. The time had come for his spiritual son to take the reins of power. As for the father of national independence, he officially withdrew from the arcane of power... so one could think.

In fact, he retained the chairmanship of the Security Council, which allowed him to maintain a certain influence on national political life, while on leaving the presidency of the Republic he became a member of the Constitutional Council. Then came the first official decision of the new interim President: to rename Astana Nur-Sultan, in homage to Nursultan Nazarbayev! The message was clear: he intended to preside over the country in the continuity of what had been put in place by his predecessor. The maneuver was clever, but it did not ensure that he would be accepted by the people as the designated successor. Kassym-Jomart Tokayev took care to organize early presidential elections that gave him a comfortable majority of about 70% while the turnout was close to 80%. He certainly obtained fewer votes than his predecessor who had never won a presidential election with less than 80% of the votes cast. Kassym-Jomart Tokayev had acquired the legitimacy to ensure the political succession of the country. In the West, for those who followed the affair, the cause was understood for Kazakhstan: the new President was going to follow in the footsteps of his predecessor who continued to keep a close eye on the management of the country. Thus, everything went smoothly.

When the events unfolded, we initially feared that various powerful people in the country would seek to gain power by any means. Indeed, there are several very powerful families in Kazakhstan that were not especially known to be close to the Nazarbayev clan. That is why we were dreading the day when Nursultan Nazarbayev would leave power. Nevertheless, everything had been meticulously prepared. The day after his resignation was announced, his daughter Dariga took over the chairmanship of the Senate. He managed to get his nephew Samat Abish a prime position by making him first vice-president of the country's intelligence services. Clearly, while he was no longer officially the all-powerful President, he had managed to retain a great deal of influence in the institutional life of Kazakhstan. Everything converged so that the political transition would take place under the best conditions.

Then the unthinkable happened in May 2020. By presidential decree, amid the Covid-19 health crisis, Dariga Nazarbayeva was dismissed from her position as President of the Senate. No official explanation was given. It was a thunderclap. Never had a President of the Senate of

Kazakhstan been dismissed by the President of the Republic in this way. Moreover, no one had ever dared to humiliate a member of the Nazarbayev clan in this way. Thus, what was going on? Did the President of the Republic suddenly want to show that he was the boss and that he did not intend to govern with the omnipresent shadow of the Nazarbayev family?

In the West, the question that arose was to try to understand the reasons for such a dismissal. The first idea that emerged was that Kassym-Jomart Tokayev was in the process of cleaning up his country to take serious control of it and to discourage anyone from getting too close to the arena of supreme power. Meanwhile, the head of the National Security Committee (the intelligence services) was none other than Karim Massimov, in office since 2016. The latter had the distinction of being also very close to Nursultan Nazarbayev since he was his head of government twice. This precision is important because he will be dismissed on January 5, 2022, and arrested three days later... This occurred a few days after the scuffles and other protests in the Caspian region because of rising gas prices. But everything happened at high speed. The protests reached Almaty, a city far from the Caspian Sea. Thus, Kazakhstan was in the international news in the first days of 2022 with rising gas prices, popular protests, and an escalation of violence in the country's major cities. Add to this an order from the President of the Republic to the armed forces to shoot into the crowd to restore order, an appeal to Russia to send military troops to assist, and the arrest of the head of the intelligence services while Kassym-Jomart Tokayev definitively ousted Nursultan Nazarbayev from his position as head of the Security Council... Sprinkle in the resignation of the government, a temporary but indefinite cut-off of the Internet connection throughout the country and one has good reason to believe that a man is imposing his law with impunity! When the information was relayed in the West, the first impression was that the President of the Republic was organizing a coup in his country and that he was acquiring the necessary means to definitively remove the Nazarbayev family from power. This interpretation of the facts is unfortunately wrong. President Tokayev only restored order in a country that was indeed on the verge of chaos, but not because of rising gas prices. The explanation lies elsewhere. Obviously, the Western world did not receive the right information. More precisely, the facts reported are true, but it is the interpretation of these facts that is wrong.

What really happened

The reality is much more complex. Many confusions have been made. The unrest in Almaty is not related to the doubling of gas prices on January 1, 2022. In the Caspian region, there were indeed protests against this price increase, but the problem was resolved as soon as possible by President Tokayev. The events in Almaty, where scenes of great violence were reported, were not the result of a protest movement against the gas price increase. It turns out that among the demonstrators there were demanding that the Nazarbayev family leave the arena of national power once and for all. Other demonstrators had simply come to give another dimension to the chaos, by attacking the city hall of Almaty. These people had the particularity, for the most part, not to be of Kazakhstani nationality. Many came from Uzbekistan, Kyrgyzstan, or Tajikistan. Some were also known to the national intelligence services for being close to Islamist organizations. This is how the head of the intelligence services, Karim Massimov, was dismissed from his post and arrested three days later for high treason. These agitation operations were ultimately prepared in the shadows to try to destabilize the regime from inside. The protests on the Caspian coast were in fact only a pretext to set the powder keg on fire in Almaty. Several sources confirmed that the agitators had been present in the country's former capital for several weeks, which would tend to confirm the thesis that the upheavals at the beginning of the year were planned. They simply had to find the right motive to legitimize them. This view is not the one presented by the Western media.

When the latter reported a request from President Tokayev to have Russian troops intervene on his territory, the first reaction was to consider it a great opportunity for Vladimir Putin to invest in Kazakhstan. In other words, it was imagined that Kazakhstan would suffer the same fate as Ukraine. To support this thought, one must recall the electric context on the Ukrainian border where the Russians and NATO are playing cat and mouse. As for Kazakhstan, the context is different. President Tokayev has activated a provision of a multiparty political-military agreement founded in 2002, the Collective Security Treaty Organization, which includes Russia, Kazakhstan, Armenia, Belarus, Kyrgyzstan, and Tajikistan. The military intervention requested by the President of the Republic was justified insofar as it was important to ensure the integrity of the territory, to maintain peace but also to fight against terrorism. In the background, Western interpretations were undoubtedly influenced by facts that we are not accustomed to impose in our countries, such as the cutting of the Internet connection or the order given to the security forces to "shoot to kill". When it was stated that Moscow supported Kassym-Jomart Tokayev, the shortcut was to consider that Vladimir Putin was supporting a dictator and that it was a way to taunt his detractors, once again in the midst of a sensitive context regarding Ukraine. No, the President of Russia only responded favorably to a head of state requesting aid justified by a multilateral treaty. The order given to the police to shoot to kill caused outrage in the West, since the first idea was to fear a bloodbath decided in order to ensure the extended power of the President of the Republic. The forces of law and order did indeed shoot. There were deaths and many arrests. Some were probably people in the wrong place at the wrong time. That is possible. On the other hand, most of the victims were actually targeted by law enforcement. In any case, the scenes of chaos in Almaty were confined to the Republic Square area. It should not be assumed that the city was under siege or even war. The images of the riots that circulated in the media did inspire concern that the escalation of tensions was no longer under control. Moreover, where the Western world expressed its indignation, Vladimir Putin and Xi Jinping did not fail to welcome the decision of President Tokayev to restore order in this way. As for Nursultan Nazarbayev, he curiously disappeared from circulation for several days. On January 19, 2022, he appeared in the national media to announce his retirement from the country's political affairs. This also implied that his family clan had decided to do the same and to withdraw from the economic business where they were very well established. [11] A chapter of national history had probably just been closed. This public appearance announced the end of the tensions that had arisen some time before. It was probably the result of a negotiation between the Nazarbayev clan and the country's authorities concerning a definitive withdrawal from political and economic life in exchange for a waiver of legal proceedings by the state. Clearly, all this puts an end to a dramatic episode that actually consisted of an attempt to bring down the President of the Republic. It turns out that the instigators have failed. Kassym-Jomart Tokayev did not give in to panic and restored order. This is the way to understand the chaotic events that shook Almaty and more globally

---

[11] Emmanuel Grynszpan, *"Au Kazakhstan, Nazarbaïev réapparaît pour annoncer sa retraite"*, www.lemonde.fr, January 19, 2022

Kazakhstan at the beginning of the year 2022. We must also understand that Russia and China were undoubtedly well informed about what was being planned against the presidency of the Republic. Their support for Kassym-Jomart Tokayev was only a reflection of a convergence of interests to be defended, especially in terms of security. In short, the Nazarbayev clan has been dropped by its former allies. Nursultan Nazarbayev had maintained excellent diplomatic relations with Russia and strengthened both diplomatic and economic relations with China. As for President Tokayev, he overcame an internal crisis of a magnitude not seen since the country's independence. On the other hand, it is certain that his decisions have remained misunderstood in the West. In any case, they will have an impact on the geopolitics of Central Asia.

Geopolitical issues disrupted

The events of early January should not make us forget that Central Asia remains a largely unknown region in the West but for which it is preferable to understand the major issues at stake. Indeed, it is a large geographical area which includes the former Soviet republics of the zone but also Afghanistan which borders Turkmenistan, Uzbekistan, and Tajikistan. Is it necessary to precise that this country, which has been at war for nearly five decades, shares borders with Iran and Pakistan? By presenting things in this way, one has a small concentrate of the many problems that make this region undoubtedly one of the most sensitive on the planet. It was therefore necessary that Kazakhstan does not fall into chaos. It is a regional power, whether it is political or economic. Moreover, the events of January 2022 occurred only a few months after the eventful withdrawal of the West from Afghanistan. It is therefore an area where the Western world has lost influence. The two main winners in the restoration of order in Nur-Sultan and Almaty are therefore Moscow and Beijing. There was no hypocrisy in the two capitals supporting the decisions of President Tokayev. By acting as he did, he undoubtedly sent a message to organizations close to terrorist movements that Kazakhstan would continue its efforts to prevent the proliferation of extremist networks within its borders. This is good for its Russian and Chinese neighbors. Beyond this consideration, it is the whole of the great game of Central Asia that is disturbed, while the local atmosphere has been quite agitated by the return in force of the Taliban in Afghanistan.

We must not conceal a detail that is important: the geopolitical cards are being reshuffled in the region. The power of influence of Europe and North America seems destined to diminish to the benefit of Russia, which, by intervening to support the action led by President Tokayev, will undoubtedly try to regain more of the influence lost in part because of the massive Chinese investments that had brought Nur-Sultan closer to Beijing. Kazakhstan is turning the page after twenty-eight years of absolute rule by the Nazarbayev clan. With the exception of Kyrgyzstan, where no clan had ever managed to take control of the country in the long term, the other former Soviet republics in Central Asia were all led by strong leaders who aimed to maintain order. In Kazakhstan, there was a fear of a complicated succession like the one in Uzbekistan after the death of its leader Islam Karimov. This gave rise to a real internal settlement of accounts, but which took place within the ruling elites. The sulphureous daughter of the deceased president, Gulnara, was immediately in the sights of the country's new decisionmakers. This had the effect of calming the ardor of those who would have liked to get involved in the jousting for power. In Kazakhstan, there were some similarities in that President Tokayev decided in 2020 to remove the daughter of Nursultan Nazarbayev from power. This was a strong gesture that suggested to the clan of the former head of state that a new era was coming to Kazakhstan and that the transmission of power would not be dynastic. Since then, it would seem that there has been a lot of secret intrigue in the arcane of national power, also involving the national intelligence services, and that something was in the works. The problem is that it all came at a sensitive time in a region where the slightest spark could have wide-ranging repercussions. Clearly, the most likely scenario was that the Nazarbayev family would find a way to compromise President Tokayev, who had been harming them since 2020. The latter was obviously smarter.

The fight against the growing terrorist threat
One of the main scourges of Central Asia is the threat of terrorism. Of course, as soon as one associates this region with terrorism, the first thought goes to Afghanistan. It would be far too simplistic to limit this risk to the jurisdiction now ruled by the Taliban. The problem with the region is that the borders are porous. It is easy for ill-intentioned networks to move around. More prosaically, there is an arc from Iran to China's Xinjiang within which it is relatively easy for terrorist movements to move. In other words, the area to be monitored is huge. As for the topography of the terrain, it obviously favors those who seek to move around discreetly. Afghanistan, Kyrgyzstan, and Tajikistan are in fact mostly composed of desert and high mountain areas. When one knows the reasons that led President Tokayev to order the police to fire on the crowd, one must understand the regional context of the fight against terrorism. In Kazakhstan, this was one of the priorities of former President Nazarbayev. The latter had fiercely fought against any form of terrorist threat. At the time, the Kazakh authorities were suspicious and were already monitoring the activities of Islamist networks that were beginning to spread in the Almaty region in particular, in the South of the country. They did not want the country

to be confronted with a growing phenomenon that they would eventually no longer control. Ironically, the man arrested for allegedly bringing in Islamist sympathizers to agitate Almaty and labelled as a terrorist by the regime was none other than Karim Massimov, the head of the intelligence services, who twice served Nursultan Nazarbayev as Prime Minister. It is noteworthy that the former head of the government comes from the Uyghur ethnic group, the same one that is being fought in neighboring Xinjiang by China.

In the Western media, a few days after the riots in Almaty, reference was made to an official communication from the Kazakh authorities about an anti-terrorist operation. Generally, the information, as relayed in the West, seems rather doubtful of the official version, preferring thus to evoke this operation with caution or even an orientation that suggests to the recipient of the message that the official justifications are to be taken with a grain of salt.

Once again, let's take a look at the course of events and the way everything was presented in the Western media. The general impression was that of an internal coup d'état perpetrated by the President of the Republic to definitively put aside the Nazarbayev clan. In other words, the famous anti-terrorist operation was only a pretext to justify the repression in the streets and the arrests of several hundred people during and after the events in Almaty. For us Westerners, this presentation of the surrounding context makes sense. It is indeed a credible scenario. The problem is that Kazakhstan is already fiercely fighting terrorism, and several of those arrested, including Kazakh citizens, were known to be fighting alongside organizations that continue to disrupt the precarious balance in the Middle East. Second, are we to believe that China and Russia supported

President Tokayev's crisis management simply out of a spirit of contradiction with the Western world? If we answer yes, it is because we do not know the regional problems. Russia and China are countries that firmly combat any form of terrorist threat. Kazakhstan shares borders with these two Eurasian giants. When Russia sees the return of the Taliban to Afghanistan and the return of Central Asian fighters who supported terrorist organizations, it obviously does not want them to gain influence in Kazakhstan and then spread to Russian territory. As for China, it is fighting the Uyghurs in Xinjiang, which it denounces as a terrorist threat. Although the West blames China for its relentlessness against the Uyghur people, the country nevertheless experienced an unprecedented wave of terrorist attacks in Beijing and Xinjiang in 2013 and 2014. [12] This is what "legitimized" the leadership's move to intensify the fight against terrorism and extremism in the Western part of the country, which also borders Kazakhstan. Both Russia and China have experienced waves of terrorism attributed to Islamist organizations. This is what makes both of them look closely at the crisis management in Kazakhstan. This is probably the main reason for the approval of the orders given by President Tokayev to the law enforcement agencies. These decisions are criticized in the West because we are not used to this kind of crisis management. The way of doing things is shocking. In these regions, the vision or the apprehension of things is different. It is not for us to pass any judgment on the decisions taken by the Presidency of the Kazakh Republic. We just wanted to bring some clarifications regarding a complex situation, for which many factual information have been spread but for which the analysis was not always good.

---

[12] Marc Julienne, *"La lutte contre le terrorisme et l'extrémisme au Xinjiang : quelles méthodes pour quels résultats? Etat des lieux et perspectives"*, www.sciencespo.fr, 2019

Conclusion

At the beginning of this year, in view of the news and the way it was reported, we suddenly had the impression that Kazakhstan was moving dangerously towards a civil war. Popular protests increasing in intensity, strict repression, arbitrary arrests, internal political tensions, foreign military intervention, resignation of the national government, all these elements combined made us fear the worst. For several days, all internet connections were cut in the country, which had the effect of isolating it. For several days, we did not have any news from our friends, noticing that they had not been able to read the messages we had sent them. The anxiety was growing. What was Kassym-Jomart Tokayev doing? According to the information circulating in the media, the impression was that of a coup d'état orchestrated by the President of the Republic himself in order to eliminate any form of threat, i.e., the clan of his predecessor. All the ingredients were present to understand things in this way.

Nevertheless, when one knows Central Asia, its history and its peoples, something was not right. Moreover, Russia and China had supported President Tokayev's management of the crisis. Was this just a provocation to the Western world? We could have thought so, but it was not the case. These two Eurasian giants sincerely supported the presidential action and thus showed their distance from the former national leader, Nursultan Nazarbayev. In reality, the situation in Kazakhstan was much more confused than what was presented in the Western media.

It was important for us to contextualize this crisis, to evoke the history of the country, that of the Soviet era and then that of national independence. It was important to understand what Central Asia is, to explain the major regional geopolitical issues but also the struggles for influence that involve the greatest political and economic powers on the planet. It was important to show how Kazakhstan, in view of its geographical position and the abundance of its natural resources, has been forced to manage its diplomatic relations with subtlety, while at the same time ensuring that order is maintained within the country due to ethnic tensions that could at any moment degenerate and produce a dangerous escalation of tensions. The Western world is largely unaware of this.

Not only does Kazakhstan occupy a central position in this region of Asia, but it is important that it does not fall into chaos because of the high risk of local problems spreading to the surrounding countries. But problems can spread very quickly. For many years, our fear has been about the post-Nazarbayev period. What would happen to Kazakhstan after the charismatic leader left power? Would he have taken care of the political transition, or would there be a terrible struggle between ambitious personalities? This was a legitimate question. Many Kazakhs had only known Nursultan Nazarbayev as head of state. In the West, we do not imagine enough the trauma that the natural or forced departure of a leader, whether a democrat or an authoritarian, causes in a population. We remember the images of people mourning the death of dictators who contributed to the death of many individuals. Is this mourning marked by a barely concealed hypocrisy? No. It is sincere. Although many have suffered from the decisions of the political regime, the loss of a leader, especially in authoritarian systems, is experienced as a real trauma that can be likened to the following question: what will become of us now? It is a real loss of reference points that takes place within society and the collective expression of a future fear. When the political transition is unprepared or poorly secured, the risks of tipping over into chaos are all the higher. This was our fear for Kazakhstan.

It came as a great surprise when Nursultan Nazarbayev publicly announced that he was officially stepping down from the presidency of the Republic with immediate effect. This announcement sounded like a warning shot. After the surprise effect, with a few days of hindsight, it appeared to us that this decision seemed well thought out and that it augured a meticulously prepared political transition. The emblematic father of independence, although aging, did not give the impression of being unwell. Also, by immediately becoming a member of the Constitutional Council and retaining his position as head of the Security Council of Kazakhstan, we understood that he was not disappearing completely from business. Officially, he was no longer the boss, but he was not leaving the arcane of power. This feeling was reinforced when his daughter Dariga immediately became the President of the Senate. In other words, she was made the number two in the regime. The acting President, Kassym-Jomart Tokayev, was close to the Nazarbayev clan. The conclusion was that while the old lion seemed to be stepping aside, he had carefully prepared for his departure so that his clan could retain the levers of political and economic power in the country. However, this meticulous preparation was not without risks. First, Dariga Nazarbayeva was not the most popular personality in the family clan. In addition, a rumor started to spread in Nur-Sultan that the daughter and the father had started to have disagreements while she was supposedly scheduled to take over the leadership of the country. In sum, this was similar to the Karimov clan in Uzbekistan, where the daughter Gulnara had set herself up against her own father. In Kazakhstan, the situation was different. At the time of the alleged tensions, Dariga Nazarbayeva was still a deputy in the Majilis. Eventually, she became the country's deputy prime minister before being elected to the Senate and enjoying a rising political career that culminated in the presidency of that parliamentary chamber. Indeed, she was the designated successor of Nursultan Nazarbayev. Secondly, in order to succeed her father, the interim President had to give her the opportunity. Kassym-Jomart Tokayev organized presidential elections in June 2019, which he won... two and a half months after the announcement that Nursultan Nazarbayev had stepped down from his executive duties. There were two possible interpretations: either the scenario was agreed upon and Dariga Nazarbayeva would patiently bide her time while maintaining her family's power of influence in the country's political and economic life; or the new President-elect had expressed the firm intention of becoming the real boss of Kazakhstan. In retrospect, the second assumption was probably correct. When he became the interim President, he inherited the prerogatives of public power from his predecessor. The President of the Republic of Kazakhstan is the strongman of the system. This is provided for in Article 2 of the national Constitution. All the difficulty consisted then in maneuvering skillfully. It was unthinkable to suddenly remove the Nazarbayev clan from power. It was risky and undoubtedly dangerous for the country's socio-political stability. It worked in fits and starts. Dariga Nazarbayeva was imposed on him as the regime's number two. But he knew how unpopular she was. When she was removed from the presidency of the Senate in May 2020, it was a huge surprise because the Nazarbayev family was being touched. Worse, it had never been done under the presidency of Nursultan Nazarbayev. Kassym-Jomart Tokayev wanted to show his authority and indicate to the people that he was not subject to any form of influence. However, when he officially took over the country, the dominant impression in the West was that of an elected man playing the role of an executor of orders received earlier. He was said to be a diplomat and not so ambitious as to want to take charge of his country's destiny. To this day, we are convinced that he never intended to be a puppet head of state.

Considering this account of Kazakhstan's recent political history, we can better understand that the chaotic events of January 2022 were not solely the result of this story of rising gas prices. It was indeed the subject of protests, but they did not degenerate into riots. The popular demands were taken into consideration by the presidency of the Republic, which was aware of the economic reality that was unfavorable to the majority of people: the health crisis in Covid-19, the devaluation of the tenge [13] and inflation have indeed had a negative impact on many Kazakh households. In this case, the increase in gas prices was not well received in a country that is one of the world's largest producers of hydrocarbons. Once again, everything quickly returned to normal in Zhanaozen and then Aktau, the original centers of the popular protest. When the media talk about a wider spread, especially in Almaty, it is true that there were indeed scenes of rioting in the former capital. However, they were not the result of rising gas prices. The reasons were different.

In the introductory section, we mentioned the reactions of several Western European countries. The main thing we remember is precisely the lack of knowledge of the country, of its current political situation, but above all of the causes that led to this state of affairs. To understand the present, one must first know the history. A huge shortcut was made between the disputes that occurred on the Caspian coast and those that agitated Almaty. It was tempting to say that what happened in the country's largest city was simply a continuation of the country's own irritation. But this was not the case. Decisions may have

---

[13] Author's note: the national currency of Kazakhstan

shocked the Western world and it is not our place to comment on them. If we do not believe in a coup d'état led by President Tokayev, we should rather consider that he has probably extinguished an attempted coup d'état. Secondly, we have read comments that the Kazakh chief executive has pledged allegiance to Vladimir Putin. This is not the case. Kazakhstan asked Russia and other countries involved in the Collective Security Treaty Organization to intervene with regard to the clauses of the collegially negotiated agreement. It was not a Russian military intervention to support a coup attempt orchestrated by Kassym-Jomart Tokayev. Moreover, once the riots had calmed down, the Russian troops left Kazakhstan. Finally, in view of the criticisms voiced by the Western world, it should not be surprising that the latter is losing even more influence in the region to Russia and China. All of this comes a few weeks after the Taliban's return to power in Afghanistan. For some time now, events have been unfavorable to Western interests, but the question we raise is simple: has anyone taken the trouble to get to know and understand Central Asia?

For Afghanistan, the Western presence was explained by the terrorist attacks of 9/11 for which an international coalition was organized to fight against the instigators. After twenty years of presence, the situation is bitter. The country has not been pacified and the departure of the Westerners was carried out under conditions that were as tumultuous as they were humiliating, with the return in force of those who were driven out of power in 2001. As for Kazakhstan, the story is obviously different. The European and American reactions to the events of January 2022 show a great ignorance of the problems of Central Asia. Serious events have just taken place in Kazakhstan. However, the image that characterizes this crisis is that of the end of a chapter in a book. Indeed, a page has just been turned in the national history: the Nazarbayev family is definitely no longer in charge of the country. A final operation tried to compromise President Tokayev by destabilizing him, but it failed. As for Moscow and Beijing, both capitals were well informed of the reality of the situation, and this is probably what led them to support the decisions of the President of the Republic for all the reasons we have mentioned in this reflection. All of this should strengthen diplomatic and economic ties between Kazakhstan and its two major neighbors.

A real risk of war in Ukraine?
Ukraine-Russia yes, Russia-NATO no
February 2022

This beginning of the year 2022 is definitely very eventful in the Russian-speaking space. While the first days of January saw a worrying agitation in Kazakhstan for obscure reasons other than those officially stated and concerning the sudden increase in gas prices, Ukraine is once again making news and sending shivers across the European continent. The risk of a war between Russia and NATO has never been so high... For several weeks, Moscow has indeed sent troops to the border areas, more than a hundred thousand soldiers or even more, while the Atlantic alliance has also massed troops near Ukraine to prevent any kind of Russian invasion. The rhetoric on both sides is offensive and intimidating. Whoever attacks will face retaliation. Everyone wants to be intransigent and inflexible. In February 2022, French President Emmanuel Macron traveled to Moscow and then to Kiev to meet separately with his Russian and Ukrainian counterparts in an effort to defuse a crisis that continues to escalate. In the media, the climate is presented as anxiety-provoking. The general tone suggests that the outbreak of an armed conflict is a possibility for which we must be prepared. In short, the situation is serious.

We still have in mind this striking image of the Putin-Macron meeting where the two men are parleying while sitting at an immaculately white and disproportionately large table that leaves the impression that the atmosphere is icy. The media provides an answer to this distancing: President Macron would have refused to submit to a test for Covid upon his arrival in Russia. This is what would have led to this precaution of leaving several meters of distance during his interview with Vladimir Putin. This image has made the rounds of the world. The two men are face to face but six meters apart while their discussions continued for five hours. There are obviously more pleasant settings for conducting diplomatic operations! This staging was undoubtedly motivated by Emmanuel Macron's refusal to pass a Covid test. That said, even without this incident, it is not excluded that the interview would have taken place under similar conditions. Vladimir Putin is a fine strategist. The conditions proposed for this sensitive discussion are intimidating. No doubt he tried to shake the confidence of his French alter ego who came to Moscow to try to ease a crisis for which he is wearing several hats: that of representative of France, the European Union (EU) but also of NATO. The man, although he has not yet officially announced it, will probably run for a second presidential term in April 2022. It is therefore important for him to look good on the international stage while he faces new popular protests in France. Similarly, since the UK's withdrawal from the EU, the two main political and economic engines are Germany and France... but Emmanuel Macron must now deal with a Chancellor who has taken over a country that was led for sixteen years by Angela Merkel, a period during which she largely proved herself on the international stage. In short, he has taken on the role of standard-bearer in a diplomatic appeasement operation at a time when the situation suggests an escalation of tensions... We must give him credit for this courageous move. But did all this require these discussions? If Russia and NATO are testing each other and the threats are serious, does either side have an interest in provoking a war with uncertain consequences that will certainly penalize all the forces involved? Our answer is very clear: we do not believe in a war scenario. More clearly, we do not believe in the scenario of a Russia-NATO war. The same is not true for Russia and Ukraine.

It's time to do some explaining because when you look at the media news, it's alarming. However, we should not confuse facts with trends. Occasional events may indeed suggest that tensions are escalating and that it may lead to the point of no return, the war. Both sides have much more to lose than to gain by engaging in an armed conflict that would benefit no one. The resentments between the two sides are tenacious. The Western world accuses Russia of many evils: espionage, cyberattacks, non-respect of human rights, undermining democracy, interference, etc. Since the beginning of the Ukraine-Russia affair in 2013, relations between Moscow and the Western world have continued to be distant. Moreover, Russia has been hit by economic sanctions. This favored a change of diplomatic and commercial course on the part of Russia, which then turned more willingly to China. It was above all the expression of a country that did not intend to be intimidated on the international scene. We remind you of this implicit but immutable rule of international relations: always seek to weaken the opponent. In the crisis between Russia and the Western world, the one who will have the attitude of a yielding party will lose credit on the international scene. Thus, an operation to de-escalate tensions is necessary to show that discussions involve pragmatic leaders while no one has an interest in provoking a war scenario. In sum, NATO and Russia are jockeying for position, flexing their muscles, and engaging in intimidating and threatening communications to show that neither will yield to any pressure or blackmail from the other side. However, it must be kept in mind that the science of conflict is unfortunately not an exact science, and that any situation can evolve in an unexpected way, positively or negatively. This is why we do not completely exclude the scenario of a war in Ukraine, which remains however very unlikely. We are witnessing a tug of war that is fully in line with the reality of international relations: the world is deeply divided. By division, we must understand that it is divided into several poles of influence, three of which are dominant: the United States accompanied by its allies, Russia, and China. On the Western side, it is important to show a union, a cohesion that should symbolize a collective strength, while the last few years have rather worked against it. The Trump presidency marked a distancing within this alliance. The Brexit was and remains a painful episode in the history of European construction. How can we not mention the Covid-19 health crisis, which was detrimental to many Western states that had not prepared for such a long crisis? On the Russian side, it is important to position oneself on the international scene while taking into consideration the recent difficulties encountered by the Western world, while there is a growing rivalry between the United States and China. Finally, on the Chinese side, the health crisis seems to have been officially digested. Vladimir Putin is being welcomed in Beijing, a few days after the Chinese New Year festivities, just before he meets with Emmanuel Macron in Moscow. The Russian head of state had come to attend the opening ceremony of the Winter Olympics in Beijing ... but also to talk with President Xi Jinping about NATO. Both are opposed to an enlargement of the Atlantic alliance. Beyond these considerations, the image conveyed by China is generally that of a serene country that intends to pursue what is led by Xi Jinping. In other words, the country is pursuing its objectives and intends to achieve them without worrying about its competitors. One calmly observes the heated exchanges between the Western world and Russia. After all, this is good for Beijing's business.

Russia wants to make its voice heard on the international scene. That is why it communicates from time to time about its desire to conquer the North Pole. The purpose of this communication is to provoke adversity, to see what the recipients of the message intend to do. The logic is similar for Ukraine. Where Russia has sent troops to island and desert areas of the Barents Sea to signal a human presence in the region, it is sending troops to the Ukrainian border to show that it can indeed envisage an invasion scenario of the Ukrainian neighbor. For this reason, NATO retaliates by massing troops around Ukraine. As soon as military personnel and armaments are mobilized, there is indeed cause for concern. The differences between Moscow and the Western world are numerous and some of them are old. It should be borne in mind that the Kremlin is analyzing the evolution of the US-China rivalry as well as the diplomatic rapprochement with the EU by President Biden. The same is true for NATO, which is moribund after the fiasco of the evacuation of Afghanistan, and which needs a sacred union within itself after this negative experience. Russia is aware of this reality.

Similarly, any pretext is good for creating misunderstandings and misinterpretations that will only contribute to the ambient malaise. We had another glimpse of this when Russia responded favorably to Kazakhstan's request to send troops to this Central Asian republic in order to resolve an insurrectionary problem that was threatening the country's socio-political stability. Russia was accused of rushing into Kazakhstan for obscure reasons, while Moscow was only responding favorably to the clause of a multilateral treaty to which Russia and Kazakhstan belong. Moreover, Moscow withdrew its troops only a few days after deploying them in the sensitive areas. The truth is that the dialogue between Russia and the Western powers is difficult. This is a certainty. But is it a dialogue of the deaf? No. On the contrary, it is all part of the power games that characterize international relations. This is the angle from which this new Ukrainian crisis should be viewed. You will understand that this new crisis does not come unexpectedly but that there are many reasons why it is happening now.

In a global environment where everyone tries to exist in their own way, there are different categories of weight or a kind of implicit hierarchy in international relations. Indeed, not all state actors influence international relations in the same way. Those who have a great power of influence are rare. It is generally the richest and best armed countries that manage to make their voices heard the most. However, within this "elite" there is yet another subdivision in which a few powers are almost always at the heart of the great international intrigues: the USA, China, Russia, and the EU. This does not mean that everything is governed by these four actors, but major crises or tensions generally involve them. The Ukrainian crisis is no exception to this rule. Russia is at the heart of the stakes, but the EU is directly concerned insofar as most of its member states are members of NATO. As soon as the Atlantic organization is mentioned, it goes without saying that the United States is directly concerned by the matter. China, on the other hand, has a different approach. It does not intervene to give advice or to try to influence any de-escalation of tensions. No. Its intervention is more subtle: it shows up on Russia's side to signal that it was not in favor of NATO expansion. The Ukrainian crisis is therefore a very concrete case of the reality of current international relations.

In the background, however, it appears that beyond state rivalries, we are witnessing above all the expression of a real clash of civilizations, which is materializing through a cultural clash and a clash of dialogue. As indicated in the introductory section, the Ukrainian crisis shows once again that States are playing a game, sometimes a dangerous one, which consists of intimidation and even threats. Sometimes this game can get out of hand and lead to armed conflict. In the case of Ukraine, despite the media's worrying and even alarmist headlines, everything seems to be under control on the side of the belligerents involved. The media relay factual information that suggests a certain level of seriousness of the situation. When Western heads of state talk about the risk of a Russian invasion of Ukraine, for which an armed response would be implemented, there is obviously reason to feel worried. However, although the risk of an armed conflict is not totally ruled out, it is an unlikely scenario. Each side seeks to intimidate the other. It is a way of wanting to expose its strength to the world. It is also a way of embodying the spirit of an old Latin saying, *si vis pacem, para bellum*, which can be translated as: if you want peace, prepare for war. It is therefore the principle of armed peace. However, the major military maneuvers carried out by Russia and NATO are not reassuring. Tensions remain high and they highlight these cultural differences which result in a difficult dialogue. In sum, the principle of armed peace is the main guarantee of an avoidable war in the Ukrainian crisis.

Yet the principle outlined above is not a wager that tensions will remain only at this stage of intimidation. It is based on a theorization that there is no outbreak of armed conflict in most cases. In mid-February 2022, the escalation of tensions is becoming increasingly critical. Bombings occurred in Eastern Ukraine, close to the border with Russia. The armed opposition involves the Ukrainian army and pro-Russian separatists. A few hours earlier, President Putin had ordered the withdrawal of Russian troops positioned on the border with Ukraine. We are thus confronted with a typical case of a critical situation that effectively suggests that the worst can happen. On the Western side, the fear is still that the Russian army will invade Ukrainian territory. However, the Russian head of state had communicated in the sense of appeasing the situation by ordering the withdrawal of troops in the border areas. In the opposing camp, the tone is different: the communication is based on a high risk of Russian intervention, in which case they are preparing for a response. In the media of NATO member countries, the main message conveyed is that of an ever-increasing risk of a degeneration of tensions with Russia. This is precisely what has led Presidents Macron and Putin to meet once again to agree on a common policy to reduce the risk of war.

This is how we view Samuel Huntington's thesis on the clash of civilizations. [14] It is the one we refer to most in our analysis of international relations. The thesis defends the coexistence of different civilizations and the multipolarity of the world. In our opinion, this is what characterizes the Russia-NATO opposition in the Ukrainian crisis. Although Russia does not intend to yield to any form of diplomatic pressure, it is nonetheless pragmatic. It is sending troops to the Ukrainian border. Thus, it shows its interlocutors that nothing intimidates it. On the other hand, when tensions reached a level that gave rise to fears of a loss of control of the situation, Moscow decided to ease the crisis by withdrawing its troops from the border areas. On the NATO side, the challenge is to avoid the outbreak of a war, but it must be understood that the interests of the heads of state of its members may differ. When President Macron engages in a dialogue with his Russian counterpart, he represents a collective voice. However, while the French head of state advocates reasonable diplomacy, his American alter ego does not hesitate to evoke a bellicose reaction in case of an invasion of Ukraine by the Russian army. The United States and France do not position themselves in the same way with respect to Russia. For Paris, avoiding a war would be a great diplomatic victory for both France and the

---

[14] Samuel Huntington, *The Clash of Civilizations and the Remaking of World Order*, Simon & Schuster, 1996, 367 pp.

EU on the international scene. The same would be true for Moscow, which would finally not play the role of the aggressor but that of a reasonable actor in international relations. In Washington, the situation is different. President Biden is facing internal tensions in the United States. He is often reproached for not being firm enough with Russia and China. He is under pressure from his detractors. There are many of them, especially among the Republicans. Thus, with regard to the Ukrainian crisis, his communication is firmer than that of President Macron. He must show that he will not be intimidated by any form of Russian action and that he is seriously considering military intervention in the event of a Russian misstep in Ukraine. In other words, Joe Biden's communication should not be seen as a deliberate attempt to add fuel to the fire on the Ukrainian issue. No, this is not the purpose of the maneuver. He is simply sending a message to Vladimir Putin. In fact, as long as this form of dialogue exists, we are convinced that there will be no war. On the other hand, it is certain that when Joe Biden mentions uncompromising reactions to Moscow in case of a Russian incursion into Ukraine, the message of the President of the United States of America is immediately relayed by all the media of the world. In other words, when the vocabulary used refers to the lexical field of war, it is normal for the media to show increasing concern. It all makes sense. As for the discussions involving Presidents Macron and Putin, they should be interpreted as a reassuring or at least encouraging sign of a bilateral will to contain tensions in Eastern Europe. However, it must be borne in mind that the risk of war is not non-existent. In such a tense situation, the slightest disturbance can be the smallest spark that no one can extinguish.

Understanding the Russian position

On February 19, 2022, tensions in the Donbass region took on a new dimension as strikes between

Ukrainian and pro-Russian separatist forces intensified. The dramatic intensity was raised another level when Secretary of Defense Lloyd Austin warned from Lithuania that Russia was *"preparing to strike Ukraine"*. At the same time, Kiev and the separatist factions accused each other of attacks. Pro-Russian leaders in the cities of Donetsk and Lugansk called for *"general mobilization"*. Vladimir Putin attended Russian military maneuvers. In Washington, Joe Biden announced that his alter ego had decided to invade Ukraine.

All this happened in the space of a few hours. When one analyzes the news over such a short period of time, the escalation of tensions is not only alarming, but everything indicates that the inevitable is going to happen. When considering the new upcoming meeting between Emmanuel Macron and Vladimir Putin, two readings are possible. First, Russia is contributing to the escalation of tensions but does not intend to provoke a war with the Western world. In other words, it can be threatening but will not intervene militarily on Ukrainian territory. Secondly, Russia has played the French President and the Western alliance by showing itself open to diplomacy and ready to engage in de-escalation of tensions... while it is preparing for war.

Once again, polemology is not an exact science. The month of February 2022 is worrying in more than one way with regard to the Ukrainian crisis because the fighting intensifies in the East of the country. It does not involve any external force since only the Ukrainian army and pro-Russian separatists are fighting. However, the evolution of events is not reassuring. We still believe that a war involving Russia and NATO will not happen because although Russia has always been firm, it has never refused diplomatic dialogue. On the other hand, it is led by a leader who has been steering it for two decades. Vladimir Putin will not act without weighing the advantages and disadvantages of the situation. He is experienced. He also knows how to antagonize NATO and circumvent the economic sanctions that have hit his country since August 2014 because of the Ukrainian crisis. Russian pragmatism is formidable. Is the Western world sanctioning Moscow? Russia then turns to China, which has every interest in ensuring its hydrocarbon supplies. A giant agreement between Eurasian neighbors was sealed. Russia sells its natural resources and China meets its energy needs. Everyone is happy. It goes without saying that no Western actor has the capacity to thwart this trade. The same is true for the geopolitics of the Arctic, a region known to have significant natural resources. For many years now, Russia has wanted to conquer and expand its influence in the region. This desire displeases the other littoral states. Moscow is pushing the vice to the point of installing military bases in isolated areas, in the northernmost latitudes of the planet. A human presence, and a military one at that, is provided to show that Russia is not playing a game of liar's poker. In reality, with regard to its Arctic ambitions, it is in a strong position as soon as global warming continues and leads to the melting of the ice caps. This will generate the creation of new maritime routes that will allow the export of hydrocarbons through routes that will get out of control of Western actors. We are thinking of maritime routes that will use the Bering Strait and that will be able to transport hydrocarbons to China. Clearly, Russia has arguments to make. A reminder is enough to underline its geographical immensity: the country shares borders with Norway and North Korea. It stretches over nine thousand kilometers and has eleven time zones. It is also for these reasons that President Putin considers the international community to be multipolar. He considers his country to be a pole in its own right. This implies that he does not intend to kneel before anyone. If he has to seal an alliance, it is a circumstantial one. He intends to restore Russia's greatness.

This will not be done at any price. He knows that an armed conflict with NATO would be catastrophic for his country. The same goes for the Atlantic alliance. Such a war would put the entire international community at immense risk. Both sides possess weapons with great destructive potential. No one could predict with certainty the victory of one side more than the other. In sum, if war were to be declared, Russia and NATO would be engaged in an open crisis that would amount to a world war. Is it in the interest of either of them to steer the debate in this direction? It would appear not.

The separatist factions are probably hoping that Russia will lend them a hand and intervene if necessary. Would Russia be willing to take this risk? No one can decide for Vladimir Putin. He is in favor of the Donbass region remaining pro-Russian. However, will he go so far as to provoke an armed confrontation that could lead to NATO action in the event of an intervention on Ukrainian territory? We prefer to think that he remains a pragmatic and strategic state leader. In this case, we are witnessing a demonstration of hard power both in Moscow and in Brussels, the headquarters of the Atlantic organization. As for the dialogue with his alter ego Emmanuel Macron, this suggests that there is still room for diplomacy and a rational agreement between Russia and NATO. Such a prospect does not necessarily imply a de-escalation of tensions between Kiev and the separatist regions. However, it may suggest that the Russian army will not intervene in Ukraine.

At the time of writing, we arrive at the end of the Winter Olympics in Beijing. President Putin had attended the opening ceremony of this great sporting event and then met with his Chinese counterpart. The two men jointly declared their opposition to NATO enlargement. We have already mentioned this. We recall that the Ukrainian crisis began in November 2013 when the national government refused to sign the association agreement linking Ukraine to the EU. This provoked the fury of many Ukrainians. This was the origin of the Euromaidan movement that started in Kiev and then spread to the main cities of the country. A few weeks later, in February 2014, the world attended the opening ceremony of the Winter Olympics in Sochi. This last one made polemic because it was question of retracing the history and the greatness of Russia. The show offered a retrospective of the great hours of the Russia of the Tsars. Then it was the turn of the Soviet era and more particularly of the industrialization of the country under Stalin. This did not fail to cause a reaction in the world because of the extreme severity shown by the little Father of the peoples. The message was very clear. Russia wanted to be impervious to any form of criticism. The spotlights were turned on it during the Olympic period, but above all, it hoped to show that nothing and no one could influence it. Moscow thus intended to assert itself as one of the dominant actors of the international relations. The Ukrainian crisis took another dimension the day before the end of the Olympic Games in Sochi, on February 22, 2014, when President Viktor Yanukovych fled and was deposed. This historical reminder is not insignificant because some analysts saw in the Beijing Olympics a sign, the one indicating that Vladimir Putin would prepare something in connection with Ukraine during the holding of the sporting event. Calendar coincidence or not, it is astonishing to note a revival of tensions in Ukraine in the middle of the Olympic period. On this point, the parallel is indeed striking. However, if Moscow has mobilized troops near the Ukrainian border, nothing proves that the real intention is an invasion and that this will lead to a domino effect with a reaction from NATO.

On February 20, 2022, President Macron reopened discussions with his Russian, Ukrainian, and American counterparts. The deterioration of the situation in the Donbass made us fear the worst. It was urgent that discussions take place in order to try to calm the situation and renew a dialogue with a view to appeasement. President Macron's initiative is remarkable in this sense since he is acting as a diplomat in the service of NATO. In 2019, in an interview with The Economist, he declared that the Atlantic alliance was brain-dead. [15] Two years later, the end of NATO's presence in Afghanistan was the event that nearly broke up the Atlantic alliance. The internal ills were not new. The organization had suffered greatly from the Trump presidency in the United States. The former White House resident had openly criticized the multiparty alliance, denouncing his country's disproportionate investment, while he considered that other member countries were not contributing enough to its budget. The end of the armed operation in Afghanistan was the last straw for an organization that was torn from within and had to suffer the affront of leaving the territory as soon as possible, driven out by those it had fought for a long time. Beyond the military fiasco, the harm was all the greater for the Western powers as it would inevitably impact their power of influence in this very strategic region of the world. Two foreign powers suddenly saw the opportunity to establish a new influence in the area: China and Russia. Some will argue that the American priority of the moment was no longer Afghanistan, but that it was important to focus on Taiwan. This is undoubtedly true, but we must not forget the discredit cast on the Western world with these evacuations, which were carried out in Dantean conditions and for which President Biden was unable to obtain any

---

[15] *"Emmanuel Macron warns Europe: NATO is becoming brain-dead"*, www.economist.com, November 7, 2019

additional time from the Taliban. President Putin has obviously kept in mind the events of August 2021 in Kabul. In his crisis management with NATO, he relies on this painful experience for the Atlantic organization and tests its cohesion. The latter must show that the Afghan episode has been digested. It is time to demonstrate that it is united and strong enough to engage in a tense arm-wrestling game with Moscow. The Russian head of state is aware of the opposition that would rise up against him if his troops invaded Ukraine. He will probably not make the mistake of underestimating it or of committing the irreparable in order to test his adversary. Given NATO's support for Kiev, a Russian incursion into Ukrainian territory would be met with an immediate response. Therefore, the scenario of an armed conflict between NATO and Russia would become inevitable. But no one wants this scenario.

The French position of proposing the use of diplomacy is an excellent initiative. Emmanuel Macron has succeeded in getting his Russian, American, and Ukrainian counterparts to engage in a dialogue to ease tensions. Once again, while this does not necessarily mean that tensions will be resolved, it is a clear sign that everyone is willing to communicate. The dialogue is therefore open. On the NATO side, it is also necessary to show indissoluble unity in view of the misjudgment of the Western world regarding the crisis in Kazakhstan a few weeks earlier. Western European chancelleries and Washington castigated the decisions taken by the Kazakh head of state, who called on Russia to send troops to Almaty in order to suppress insurrectionary movements. The latter had then given orders to the forces of order to "shoot to kill". The Western world reacted strongly by denouncing such an order, while Russia and China welcomed President Tokayev's decision. It was feared in the West that Russia would take advantage of this crisis in Central Asia to establish a new form of influence there. In the background, Russia was suspected of wanting to act with Kazakhstan as it has done with Ukraine since 2013... The cases are completely different! The intervention of Russian troops in its Central Asian neighbor was of the order of a few days. On the other hand, the support given by Moscow and Beijing to President Tokayev will undoubtedly reduce the power of influence of the Western powers that have strongly criticized the decisions of the Kazakh chief executive.

The NATO member countries and the Atlantic organization have therefore just experienced disillusionment over Central Asian issues, one of which involved a Russian intervention. All this is a factor in the Russian apprehension of the tense situation encountered with Ukraine. If NATO wants to be considered a credible military power, it must communicate in a way that will be considered seriously by the Kremlin. Above all, it must display a sacred union and a communication unanimously approved by all its members. For NATO, the stakes are high: it is a question of avoiding the outbreak of an armed conflict at the doors of several of its member countries. This is why the firmness displayed by the United States via President Biden must be considered the most logical option in view of the situation. While he is showing determination towards Russia, one actor is becoming impatient. The Ukrainian head of state Volodymyr Zelensky fears that his country will suffer the bad consequences of NATO-Russia diplomacy. In this case, he has good reason to fear such a scenario. An easing of tensions between Moscow and Brussels can only come about through a compromise based on concessions made by both sides. It is unimaginable that one side would accept concessions without a counterpart. President Zelensky has legitimate reasons to be concerned. His country will be the big loser in the talks.

If you want an argument for a war that will not break out, consider that Russia and NATO agree on one thing: they do not want common borders in Eastern Europe. The common borders between NATO and Russia are Norway, Estonia, and Latvia, plus Lithuania and Poland considering the Russian enclave of Kaliningrad. On the other hand, Finland must be added to the common borders of Russia and the EU. Finland is not a member of the Atlantic organization. In short, the land borders between Russia and NATO are of the order of a few hundred kilometers. If Ukraine were to join the organization, the situation would change, since the two countries share more than one thousand five hundred of land borders. Ukraine and Belarus act as buffer states. This configuration suits both NATO and Russia. It allows them to maintain turbulent diplomatic relations without increasing the risk of spillover precisely because of the presence of these two buffer states. On the other hand, if there are direct borders, the apprehension of tensions would be modified. Managing them would probably be more difficult. This is what has led to gas crises in the past. If Russia were to attack Ukraine or Belarus, many Central and Eastern European countries would be affected by the interruption of gas supplies from Russia. This is also the reason why the Nord Stream pipelines were built in the Baltic Sea: to allow Russia to export its natural gas to Europe while bypassing the transit through Belarus and Ukraine. For Moscow, the Nord Stream pipelines were a major asset in its fluctuating diplomatic relations with Minsk and Kiev.

The overall impression we have of this umpteenth Ukrainian crisis is that both Russia and NATO are well aware of the line that must not be crossed. Both are aware of the opposing strengths and weaknesses. When President Macron managed to obtain the consent of his American and

Russian counterparts to meet, President Biden gave his approval while imposing a condition: there will be a meeting with Vladimir Putin if Russia does not intervene in Ukraine. Once again, the Western world wants to be benevolent towards Kiev. The Ukrainian President would thus have good reasons to be reassured... However, the latter is not fooled. He knows that the internal problems of his country will not be solved by him. He will undoubtedly have a say in the matter, but he will not be the decisionmaker. He is aware of this. What matters most to him is to avoid a war on his territory. For the rest, NATO and Russia will decide.

As long as it is in the interests of NATO and Russia to maintain a buffer zone, the country concerned will suffer the consequences. In this case, Ukraine has a great tragedy: it is an independent and sovereign state, but there is not one Ukrainian nation. There are two: one is Ukrainian and the other Russian. If war is avoidable, an easing of tensions will not erase the national socio-political problems. The pro-Russian factions will never side with Kiev and the EU. The example of Crimea is telling. Although the referendum that occurred in 2014 was not recognized by the Western world, the Crimeans only showed their attachment to Russia. If such a case were to occur in the Donbass, the majority of voters would vote for the region's attachment to Russia. In sum, President Zelensky can consider two scenarios: first, to retain the national territorial integrity. In this case, he knows that part of the country will never approve of decisions by Kiev that run counter to Russia's interests. Second, Ukraine is resigned to accepting that pro-Russian regions will no longer be part of the national territory. Such a decision could generate unrest within the Ukrainian nation, which would then see a weakness in the authorities or even a form of treason. In any case, President Zelensky is inheriting a situation that is not new, since Ukraine is a country that has long been sacrificed on the stage of international relations. Although he has Western support (NATO and the EU), it is certain that he will not risk going beyond a certain limit that Russia would not accept. In principle, one denounces Russian bad actions while maintaining a measured attitude. If the game is not worth the candle, there will be diplomatic support given to Kiev without the interests of the Ukrainian capital being satisfied.

The Ukrainian drama is twofold. First, the country is geographically located in a region that acts as a buffer between two zones that maintain difficult diplomatic relations. Second, it will continue to be penalized by the mathematical inequality of "one state, two nations. The problem for the national authorities is that internal tensions cannot be resolved by the government when external actors interfere. Ukraine is and will remain a battleground for Russia and NATO-EU. This is obvious. This is why, despite the escalation of tensions that has momentarily raised fears of the worst, the scenario of a war remains unlikely, although it is not non-existent. In the meantime, diplomacy will now focus on calming tempers and finding a common ground that suits everyone.

Russia-NATO negotiations lead to status quo
President Macron has undoubtedly succeeded in convincing Joe Biden and Vladimir Putin to meet. The credit goes to him. The two men had met in Geneva a few months earlier for a summit that in the end had nothing historic about it. This is an opportunity to meet again and to discuss in a concrete way. In our opinion, they were waiting for this! What kind of discussion can we expect? We can anticipate debates that could turn stormy. In the end, each side will try to show that they got what they wanted. In other words, each side will make concessions that will not actually hurt anyone... except for Ukraine. One cannot

imagine Joe Biden or Vladimir Putin accepting conditions that are too damaging and that would later be blamed on them in Washington or Moscow. The United States will not make Russia bend and vice versa. It is all a question of calculation and balance. In this game, it seems to us that the main protagonists will be able to show pragmatism.

In sum, we expect a status quo scenario. The diplomatic crisis will ease the tensions that will still be alive in the separatist regions. However, Russians and NATO forces will agree not to have to confront each other militarily. Russian troops will be asked to move away from the borders with Ukraine. The Russians will ask NATO to keep certain weapons they do not like away from their borders. Finally, Moscow will be tempted to demand that the Nord Stream 2 pipeline be allowed to transfer natural gas to the EU. As for Ukraine, we are not taking much of a risk in saying that its membership in the EU and / or NATO will no longer be on the agenda in the coming years. Clearly, diplomacy will triumph, and Kiev will once again be the big loser. The world will salute the diplomatic efforts made by Moscow, Washington, and Brussels. Emmanuel Macron will forever remain the man without whom the crisis could have tipped over into irrationality. In short, the script is already written...

In practice, this is probably the spirit in which the diplomatic discussions will take place. Points of compromise will have to be found. This does not mean that there will be no clashes between Joe Biden and Vladimir Putin. We are just confident that they have no interest in letting the situation escalate. Again, no one has an interest in a war breaking out in this part of Eastern Europe. In terms of political communication, there is an imperative for everyone to intervene: in view of the US-Russian animosity, no head of state should give the impression to his people that he is the loser in the negotiations. It is important for each of them to show that they have obtained convincing results by displaying determination and inflexibility at all times. This is the greatest challenge of future discussions: to find common ground while giving the impression to the respective peoples that each has succeeded in asserting its interests. The worst image that can be given is that of a negotiator who has had to concede too much to adversity. This is why the future summit suggested by the French head of state will not be a mere formality. Time is needed for each party to prepare, to compile the points to be made, those that can be the subject of a concession and those, on the contrary, on which it will be necessary to show intransigence.

The big loser at the upcoming summit will be Ukraine. In the end, while Russia and NATO will do what is necessary to prevent a war from breaking out, Kiev's room for maneuver will be extremely limited. President Zelensky will be able to make his voice heard, but it is unlikely to influence the content of the multiparty agreement that will be negotiated. Kiev dreams of NATO membership, but it will not happen soon. Russia will agree to negotiate with the Atlantic alliance as soon as it is certain that the latter will not expand into Eastern Europe. NATO and the EU will continue to communicate in the sense of unwavering support for Ukraine, but the concessions that will be made to Russia will be at the expense of Kiev's interests. Russia will certainly play on this point. This hypothesis is all the more likely since Vladimir Putin and Xi Jinping had jointly declared their disapproval of seeing NATO enlarge. There was nothing innocuous about this message. It announced the tone of what was to follow: tensions continued to rise so that Moscow could negotiate for the best possible easing of tensions. As for Beijing, the message is somewhat different: it is to show the Western world that China is concerned about diplomatic affairs in Eastern Europe. China has important economic interests in Belarus. Eastern Europe is one of the geographical areas targeted by the deployment of the new Silk Roads. Finally, and this is probably the strongest message, Xi Jinping is joining forces with Vladimir Putin. The two heads of state are thus displaying an image of concord that is intended to strike a chord with NATO and the EU. When he meets Joe Biden, the Russian President will not fail to remind him that he is not the only one who is opposed to an enlargement of the Atlantic organization. All this leads us to believe that Kiev will be the main, if not the only, loser in the negotiations. Russia and NATO will get off lightly by claiming a diplomatic breakthrough that will remove the risk of war. As for Kiev, the capital will not be rid of the ills that have plagued it for so long. Unless a part of the territory obtains to be no longer part of Ukraine (which implies long and painful negotiations as well as international recognition in fine), the country will continue to be weakened by this bi-national animosity: the Ukrainian nation on one side and the Russians of Ukraine on the other. Thus, while dismissing the specter of a war between Russia and NATO, no one will focus on solving Ukraine's internal ills. Needless to say, this is the scenario feared by President Zelensky.

Chinese serenity in the face of the Ukrainian crisis
The first impression that any observer or analyst can make is that China is geographically distant from the Ukrainian troubles. In this case, if there is one world power that can be calm about the situation, it is the Middle Kingdom. If a war were to break out, there is little chance of it spreading to the far reaches of Central Asia. On the other hand, the Ukrainian crisis is not without interest for Beijing. Once again, the intervention is about not wanting to see NATO and the Aukus (a military alliance linking the

United States, the United Kingdom, and Australia. This tripartite alliance was made public in September 2021. It seeks to counter China's expansionism in the Indo-Pacific area) resounds as a warning to these military alliances and to the United States in the first place. The Ukrainian crisis is a perfect opportunity for the world's major diplomatic powers to make their voices heard and to position their pawns on the chessboard. Ultimately, it is a great game of chess. China has not failed to make it clear that it shares Russia's view on the subject. This message has a surprising dimension: it is rare for Beijing to speak out on international affairs. If the Chinese capital has acted in this way, it is not only out of "sympathy" or "friendship" towards Vladimir Putin. Xi Jinping had a message to send. He succeeded. In the West, one immediately thinks of a form of Sino-Russian alliance. The interests are multiple. China warns the West. No one will prevent it from pursuing its expansionist policy towards both the East and the West without exposing itself to a firm reaction on its part. As soon as Western military alliances are mentioned by name, it must be understood that Beijing could retaliate militarily.

China is not a completely detached spectator of the Ukrainian crisis. The reason is simple: it involves most of the world's major political and economic players. The US, Russia and the EU are all involved in this sensitive issue. The same goes for NATO. Beijing is finishing its winter Olympics in the greatest serenity: the conflicting problems of Eastern Europe are far from its lands. As for Russian provocations, the Chinese capital does not communicate much on the subject. In short, China should not be expected to condemn Russian provocations. When China officially expressed its disagreement with a future and hypothetical enlargement of NATO and the Aukus, the aim of the maneuver was clear: it was necessary to warn the Western world that it would henceforth share its opinions on the major international issues. In this case, this declaration is particularly sensitive because it is about a military alliance. In other words, it is giving its opinion on the hard power of the Western world. This means that NATO and the Aukus would obviously be wrong to take this communication lightly. Beijing's international positioning is evolving and taking a more worrying form for the Western world.

President Xi Jinping's communication is confusing in the sense that he excels in the art of conveying messages that challenge the West while maintaining his phlegm and his immutable smile. However, it must be understood that China is asserting itself in a different way. When it joins Vladimir Putin in denouncing a possible enlargement of the Atlantic alliance, it is not doing so simply at Russia's friendly request. It does so because it has an interest in doing so. It is telling the world that it does not intend to engage only in an economic battle for world leadership. It is strong enough now to give its opinion on major crises of conflict. This is new. It gives the full measure of Chinese ambitions. The Middle Kingdom is shifting the center of gravity of the world economy by projecting itself in the restoration of the Silk Roads. [16] As for political ambitions, they are now clear: Beijing will make its voice heard, just as the Western world does, on all issues for which the Chinese authorities feel the need to communicate. In other words, we are witnessing a new evolution in international relations. While China has been demonstrating its great economic ambitions for several years, it now intends to show that it is also a major player in international politics. The communication of February 4 is certainly a landmark event since it confirms the multipolarity of the world and the increase in tensions among the dominant state powers. This communication is all the more remarkable because it comes

---

[16] See Thierry Pastor, *In the shadow of Titans*, 208 pp. *Op.cit.*

on the same day as the opening ceremony of the Beijing Winter Olympics. In other words, in the midst of sporting festivities, Russia and China took advantage of the opportunity to broadcast a message about military considerations. Since then, tensions in Eastern Europe have risen. Russia has pursued an ambiguous policy marked by an openness to dialogue combined with decisions that make it increasingly sensitive. As for China, it did what it had to do on February 4. Its ambition was to deliver a message to the Western world. Everyone heard it. In this geopolitical crisis, China has always defended Moscow's positions. According to both countries, NATO is an anachronistic aberration, a relic of the Cold War that no longer exists. It goes without saying that this sentiment is not shared by its member states. Everyone now knows where they stand.

Russia's risky provocation

What is Russia playing at? This is undoubtedly the big question facing the EU and NATO players on February 21, 2022. The day before, President Putin had agreed in principle to a forthcoming summit with his American counterpart in order to find a diplomatic solution to the Ukrainian crisis. The next day, as the Western world and the United Nations began to prepare the ground for future diplomatic discussions on the topic, Moscow surprised the world by pronouncing itself in favor of recognition of the pro-Russian separatist regions of Ukraine. It is linking words to deeds by sending a division of armored vehicles to the regions of Donetsk and Lugansk. At the same time, it ordered Kiev to stop military operations against the separatist factions. The tension suddenly went up a notch. On the Western side, it was astonishment. The day before, the Russian head of state had agreed in principle to a diplomatic summit with Joe Biden to ease tensions; the day after, he torpedoed his verbal agreement by shattering the indispensable condition set by the American President for such an event: not to intervene in Ukraine. It goes without saying that the recognition of the independence of the separatist regions is not approved by the Western world. The same goes for the UN. By doing so, Vladimir Putin gives the impression that he wants to provoke an armed conflict. However, this is the umpteenth provocation aimed at testing NATO, the United States, and the EU, which immediately reacted by imposing sanctions. The UN denounced this as a violation of international law. As for the United States, they deplore the Russian will not to consider the diplomatic way. In fact, by recognizing the independence of the separatist regions and by sending armored divisions, Russia has not set any ultimatum and has proceeded to a declaration of war. Technically, this is how it should be understood.

However, the entry of Russian troops into Ukraine did not lead to an armed response from NATO. The West's initial focus is on sanctions to dissuade Russia from pursuing this initiative. Given the way Vladimir Putin has surprised the Western world, it is unlikely that these sanctions will persuade him to suddenly stop his support for the pro-Russian regions that he now recognizes as independent. The crisis has thus taken on another dramatic dimension. Hope for a diplomatic outcome is diminishing, as Russia has acted in a way that leaves little room for NATO to maneuver. The deception is all the greater since President Putin had accepted the day before President Macron's proposal to consider an ad hoc diplomatic summit for the Ukrainian crisis. In all Western chancelleries, the feeling is that of a shameless deception on the part of Moscow. The scenario seemed prepared.

On February 21, Russian television broadcast an absolutely disconcerting scene in which Vladimir Putin questioned the head of the country's foreign intelligence services. [17] He is accompanied by Prime Minister Mikhail Mishustin, Foreign Minister Sergey Lavrov and former President and head of government Dmitry Medvedev. The intelligence boss was then interrogated with stammering and stuttering answers. In the end, he declared his support, not without difficulty, for the recognition of the independence of the Donetsk and Lugansk regions. All this staging can be seen as a maneuver aimed at demonstrating Russia's determination not to bend to any Western demands. For the opposing camp, this position of the Kremlin is an affront in more ways than one. Indeed, for both the United States and the European players, the Russian about-face is a mark of contempt granted to the diplomatic efforts promoted by Emmanuel Macron as well as to Joe Biden's acceptance of being open to dialogue while imposing the condition of non-invasion of Ukrainian territory. Vladimir Putin thus intends to show that no one will impose negotiation conditions on him beforehand and that he is ready to go all the way with his ideas. Clearly, he fears nothing and nobody. He is acting to see how the opposing camp will react. Within the latter, everyone agrees to denounce the Russian attitude. What should be the collective reaction? Indeed, when talking about NATO, one should not forget the interests defended by the EU but also by the United States, independently of the Atlantic alliance. As for Russia, Vladimir Putin has just shown once again that he is the real boss of the Russian ship. He decides. The United States, through its Secretary of Defense, had indicated two days earlier that it feared a Russian invasion of Ukraine. This communication had come on the eve of the diplomatic efforts made by President Macron. For the latter, the blow must be hard because his efforts at dialogue have been destroyed by a reversal of the situation that disavows

---

[17] *"Le dialogue lunaire entre Poutine et le chef du Service des renseignements russes à propos de l'Ukraine"*, www.lefigaro.fr, February 22, 2022

him. He has, however, implemented what probably needed to be promoted in order to avoid a war.

Many questions remain. Why did Vladimir Putin act in this way? What is he trying to achieve? Our hypothesis, which may be wrong, is that he was angered by the non-negotiable condition imposed by President Biden to agree to a diplomatic summit on condition that Russia does not intervene militarily in Ukraine. The Kremlin's attitude might have been different if this condition had not been exposed. However, should we blame the President of the United States for wanting to ensure a form of non-aggression pact? His condition was not awkward. Once again, he is under great pressure in his country. He must show that he is a strong leader and that he will not be intimidated by Russia or China. The problem is that President Putin does not see it that way. By reacting as he did, he simply sent another signal to his critics that no one would impose conditions on him before an opportunity for dialogue. The Western camp is considering sanctions to be imposed on Russia. At first, the possibility of a military intervention with uncertain consequences is not mentioned. We are trying to find ways other than war to ease tensions. The problem with sanctions is that they can have the perverse effect of contributing to an unstoppable escalation. As soon as Russia announced that it was recognizing the independence of the pro-Russian separatist regions, the financial markets went into overdrive. Everyone fears a gas war. Oil trading prices are at their highest for several years. On February 22, Brent crude oil was trading above $97 a barrel, while WTI was above $92. Russia may indeed opt for a temporary halt in natural gas deliveries to Europe. This is what led Germany to declare that it was suspending the authorization of the Nord Stream 2 pipeline, which is to carry Russian natural gas to the German terminal in

Greifswald. This gas war is strangely reminiscent of some past disputes between Russia and Ukraine in the 2000s.

To date, Vladimir Putin is pushing his opponents to the limit. He is engaged in a war of nerves. He is testing them. He is trying to find out their limits. Would they risk a military response? We remain convinced that a war would not be beneficial for either Russia or NATO. However, the strong man in the Kremlin has engaged in an arm-wrestling game with an uncertain outcome, an outcome for which the power of diplomacy may, for the time being, prove powerless. He demonstrates once again that he is a master of tactics and strategy. He feels all the stronger because China agrees with him on his dislike of NATO. No one will teach him this immutable golden rule of international relations: always find a way to weaken the opponent. Today, he is bullying the Western alliance.

The need for mutual understanding
Certainly, if parties to the crisis are unwilling to dialogue, it is unlikely that the crisis will end without an official declaration of war. That would be the worst-case scenario. However, we continue to believe in diplomacy and the pragmatism of the various actors at the heart of this war of nerves. For the Western world, it is imperative to show unity in the face of Russia, which is blowing hot and cold in order to destabilize it. The good intentions of the West are not to be questioned. On the other hand, the adversary is called Russia. The latter is masterfully led by a man trained in the old Soviet school at the height of the Cold War. Vladimir Putin is inflexible, uncompromising, and icy with his detractors. He embodies the strong man, the one who does not let himself be influenced by threats. He has never closed the doors to dialogue, but he refuses any form of condition imposed for the continuation of discussions. In short, he wants to be offensive in order to

better understand what the opposing camp is ready to put in place to counter him. When he undertook to recognize the independence of several Ukrainian regions and decided to send armored divisions there, he knew that he had reached a sensitive point on the Western side. What to do? To respond with force or to show temperance and opt for a different strategy while not giving in to Russian provocations at all? Vladimir Putin has made his move. It is now up to the West to respond.

On February 22, 2022, President Joe Biden announced his intention to address the Americans. In the meantime, the Russian President reiterated his recognition of the separatists' sovereignty in the Lugansk and Donetsk regions. NATO is now convinced of an imminent attack by Russian armed forces in these areas. The Atlantic organization has put its rapid reaction force on alert. The latest news of the day is not reassuring. The dialogue seems to have broken down with Moscow.

The facts reported by the media are disturbing. When one follows the chronology of events between February 19 and 22, the conclusion is that there is a dangerous escalation of tensions heading towards a point of no return. This is the impression that emerges. Certainly, it is difficult to communicate with the Kremlin under these conditions. On closer inspection, dialogue with Russia has been difficult for several decades. One has sometimes the impression of experiencing the peaks of tension that once animated the Cold War. That time is three decades past, but the scent of that stormy period in modern international relations has never really dissipated. In the eyes of the West, Russia remains a suspicious actor, even an enemy. The nature of the opposition has changed. Vladimir Putin intends to restore the greatness of his country on the international scene and is giving himself the means to do so.

He provokes, he intimidates, he threatens. The level of provocation he indulges in can be surprising because it leaves the Western world to imagine that he is ready to do anything to get satisfaction, including the hypothesis of starting a war. When one delves into his vision of the contemporary world, he does not hide his multipolar approach to international relations. In the way he expresses it, he takes care to imply that Russia is a pole in its own right. It does not have the economic power of the US or the EU, but it has other arguments to put forward. Russia has a good military arsenal. It has natural resources that Europe covets, although Europe is considering sanctions on Moscow's energy exports. It is probably not these sanctions that will make the Kremlin hesitate. The Kremlin can count on a strong support from China. This changes the game completely. Although it is an alliance of circumstance, the Russians and Chinese know how to be formidable pragmatists when it comes to thwarting Western interests. In this case, from this point of view, their mutual interests converge.

However, this does not make the Moscow-Beijing tandem a pole in international relations. Each is a pole. In short, when we analyze the Ukrainian crisis, we realize that the Western alliance is faced with a real basic problem: the United States-EU versus Russia-China. In each camp, a political and economic giant seems more powerful than its ally. The fundamental difference is that the EU would not venture to declare war on Russia. Russia alone can start one. In other words, armed action by NATO cannot be envisaged without American intervention. Russia does not need Chinese help to engage in an armed struggle against the Western world. Moreover, it would be surprising if China were to intervene in such an armed conflict. However, the fact is that Russia is supporting where the Atlantic alliance is most vulnerable: there can be no military response without American intervention. For the time being, it is not certain that Joe Biden is inclined to mobilize his troops for a war against Russia. On the one hand, he has no certainty of winning an armed struggle against another major military power. On the other hand, a war in Eastern Europe would likely have implications for Indo-Pacific geopolitics, precisely where the Aukus alliance operates.

Not surprisingly, the February 23 press review reports on President Biden's televised speech. He said he wanted to strengthen the arsenal of sanctions against Russia. He cancelled the diplomatic summit with Russia because the latter had violated the condition he had submitted. In the United States, this intervention has above all the gift of highlighting the internal political dissensions. If CNN is content to report in a neutral way the new sanctions to come [18], Fox News wants to be much more critical by affirming that Joe Biden does not want to confront Vladimir Putin in an armed conflict [19], implying that the White House fears to engage in a war against the Kremlin. On the Moscow side, it seems that the night has brought advice. President Putin insists that his country remains open to *"direct and honest dialogue"* while specifying that everything that refers to the security of his country is non-negotiable. [20] On the surface, the tone is more conciliatory, a clear sign of a desire not to have to commit to an extreme outcome. However, this message adds fuel to the fire since it expresses a firmness, even an inflexibility. In short, it is he who sets the conditions for

---

[18] Kevin Liptak, *"Biden says Russia is beginning an 'invasion of Ukraine' as he unveils sanctions on Moscow,"* edition.cnn.com, February 22, 2022

[19] Michael Lee, *"US military firepower rushing to Ukraine as besieged nation faces Russian invasion"*, www.foxnews.com, February 22, 2022

[20] AFP, *"Poutine se dit «ouvert au dialogue» mais les intérêts russes restent «non négociables»"*, www.lefigaro.fr, February 23, 2022

dialogue with the opposing camp. His speech is also characterized by a much less peaceful reminder since he mentions the new weapons developed by Russia, some of which he describes as *"invincible"*. [21] In short, he is simply applying to the letter the old Latin saying that anyone who wants peace must prepare for war.

Dialogue with Russia will be difficult if not impossible. A war is always avoidable when people of good will show their intention not to have to fight on armed ground. The Western alliance is not standing idly by as orders have been given to position troops and armaments near the Russian border. Diplomacy can still ensure that this political crisis is reversible and that it leads to a de-escalation of tensions. This will not be an easy task. At the heart of the problem is the Samuel Huntington's thesis of the clash of civilizations and cultures. This is probably an underlying point on which Vladimir Putin relies.

Since the end of the Cold War, the international community has been largely guided or influenced by Western standards. This was only possible because of the overwhelming dominance of the Western world, led by the United States, over the world. The situation has changed considerably since then. Non-Western powers are asserting themselves on the international scene and are clearly rejecting the standards that the West is trying to impose on the world. In the name of democracy or human rights, the West has launched wars in Afghanistan and Iraq, the military results of which are not brilliant. While the coalition forces were bogged down in these areas, where they succeeded in dislodging the political leaders they were targeting, they then experienced a period of chronic socio-political instability and the rise of terrorism. All this

---

[21] *Ibid.*

undermined the credibility of Western hard power, while at the same time some countries experienced strong economic growth coupled with a qualitative and quantitative increase in their armaments. In other words, the hard and soft power of China and Russia are no longer comparable to those of the 2000s. Nowadays, these two countries can engage in an arm wrestle with the Western world and firmly oppose it, even if it means the threat of war. It is in these conditions that the civilizational and cultural clash takes on even more importance. It is a question of dealing with actors who do not share a vision of things that goes in the direction of those of the West. They no longer accept Western domination. This makes the test of dialogue more difficult. The Western world understands that it can no longer impose its views and thoughts as it pleases on Russia or China. Intimidation does not work with Moscow or Beijing. It is now time to address the issue of dialogue. Russia will never agree to engage in an attempt of diplomatic resolution where it will not be seen as the equal of the Western world. This is how Vladimir Putin is preparing the next diplomatic steps to ease the Ukrainian crisis. Once again, the world has changed. So have the codes of communication.

Conclusion

The Ukrainian crisis is a perfect example of geopolitical complexity. How does an internal problem, that of a country comprising two nations, become an issue of international concern involving the greatest political powers on the planet? This diplomatic dispute also confirms the evolution of international relations in a trend where American, and more generally Western, domination is no longer as evident as it was in the 1990s and 2000s. In saying this, we are not defending the thesis of an American or Western decline. It is more appropriate to speak of a reduction in the gap that separated the Western world from the rest of the world. Today, several states are seeing their power (hard and soft power) grow to the point of allowing them to express themselves as equals with the Western world. The quality of a country's armaments favors its positioning on the international scene. Although North Korea's economy is in a state of collapse, its nuclear weapons are feared by the international community, and it is precisely this weaponry that allows the Kim family to maintain its grip on the country. When Russia claims to possess weapons that it describes as "invincible", foreign intelligence agencies have an idea of the quality of these weapons, their power and destructive potential. Thus, a country that possesses weapons that can generate large-scale destruction will be viewed with caution by its adversaries. The more powerful the weapons, the greater their deterrent effect. Weapons are not just military weapons. Digital technology is now a major weapon for anyone who has the ability to cause harm from a distance via cyberattacks. In this case, four major geographical areas can claim to possess these two major assets: the United States, China, Russia, and the EU. The Ukrainian crisis directly involves three of them and indirectly the fourth one. Indeed, Washington, Moscow and Brussels are directly concerned by these tensions in Eastern Europe, notably because of NATO's involvement. As for Beijing, it provides political support to Russia and has publicly expressed its criticism of NATO and the Aukus, a clever and effective way to send the message that the Chinese capital is on the side of Moscow in the Ukrainian crisis.

President Zelensky has many reasons to fear the diplomatic outcome of this crisis. He will be powerless in view of the foreign forces involved in this matter. What room for maneuver can he have considering that the United States, Russia, the EU, and China are defending antagonistic interests in this Ukrainian crisis? How can he effectively play the game while the four greatest political and military powers on the planet are testing each other in a clever power game that illustrates the reality of international relations? President Putin will continue to titillate the West. He feels strong because beyond his military power, the benevolent shadow of Beijing reminds NATO that if Russia is officially engaged alone in this tension against the Western alliance, China has not failed to communicate on several occasions to express its position on the topic... In sum, despite the seriousness of the situation, this state of affairs leads us to believe that the opposition is such that it would be irrational to provoke a war. No one wants to engage in an armed conflict in which he has no certainty of winning. Russia's game is to show that it is determined to go all the way if NATO does not accept its conditions. It is therefore displaying its intransigence. The Western world was not used to such an attitude in the 1990s and 2000s. It must therefore deal with this reality. It is uncomfortable because such a situation is a novelty. Russia and China will not hesitate to use this opportunity to assert their positions and desires on the international scene. This undoubtedly explains President Biden's reaction to be measured in his communication: he announced sanctions against Moscow and the order to show readiness for military intervention. However, the tone of the speech is less offensive than that of Vladimir Putin, who wants to be much sharper. Since the end of the Cold War, the United States is no longer used to anyone standing up to it in this way. Yet this reality is not new. In 2014, when the Western world sanctioned Russia for what was already a crisis with Ukraine, Moscow turned to Beijing for huge natural gas trade deals that would allow it to make up for lost revenue with the West over time. More recently, Beijing sent a signal to Washington by sealing massive trade contracts with Iran, a country that had been ostracized by the Western powers. Worse, the United States had been threatening any ally tempted to trade with ancient Persia. China showed that it was not impressed by the intimidation of the White House. During the Trump presidency, the United States has engaged in various trade, customs, technology, and other battles with China. The latter showed no signs of weakness and responded piecemeal depending on the intensity of the sanctions against it. All this happened in the 2010s. As already mentioned in this reflection, the Western world has also been marked by its recurrent difficulties in fighting terrorism. It suffered the humiliation of leaving Afghanistan under conditions imposed by the Taliban. It misunderstood the Kazakh crisis that broke out in January 2022. All this contributed to discredit it on the international scene... while doing the business of China and Russia. Thus, the Ukrainian dispute is not happening at any time. As for the escalation of tensions, it took another turn when China gave its support to its Russian neighbor. Under these conditions, it is not surprising that Vladimir Putin acts in this way, raising the specter of provoking a war. He is playing a score for the sole purpose of finding out what his opponents are up to. For a long time, no one has ventured to act in this way with the players who dominate the world's hard and soft power.

International relations will be tense. Everything will be a pretext to show a competitive spirit, to show who is the strongest. If there is a country to be pitied in this context, it is Ukraine. If it is not true to say that the country is not considered in the media, it is above all the Russia-NATO opposition that is highlighted. In other words, the fate of Kiev is almost relegated to the background. At the time of writing, no one knows what will happen to Ukrainian unity. Russia has struck a blow by recognizing the independence of the Donetsk and Lugansk regions. It is certain that the opposition will refuse to accept such recognition. These separatist regions will continue to be a source of tension. If Kiev and NATO were to recognize this independence, it would obviously be a great victory for Russian diplomacy and a political tour de force that would leave a lasting impression. As for the need to maintain a buffer zone in Eastern Europe between Russia and NATO, it is more relevant than ever. It is therefore logical that Moscow should demand that Ukraine not join the Atlantic alliance. On this point, the Kremlin has good reason to expect satisfaction. Despite the fact that the risk of a Russia-NATO war has not been eliminated, we remain convinced that it will not happen. There are too many leading belligerents in opposition. Realpolitik, which Henry Kissinger defined as *"foreign policy based on the calculation of forces and the national interest,"* [22] will prevail. However, it will only reinforce this sense of the world's multipolarity and the narrowing of power levels among the dominant states or political groupings. To paraphrase the title of a famous work by Jean Giraudoux, *The Trojan War will not take place.* As for Kiev, the city will continue to be the sacrificed capital in Eastern Europe. It will be that intermediate zone that will allow both sides not to share land borders in this sensitive region. Despite the support of the EU and NATO, the country will continue to evolve with the internal ills that make it so fragile. Indeed, if diplomacy hopes to achieve a favorable outcome between Moscow, Washington and Brussels, the Ukrainian state will remain weakened by this bi-national context marked by pro-European Ukrainians on the one hand and pro-Russian Ukrainian citizens on the other. In other words, if the tensions between Russia and NATO can be reduced (the effect would probably be temporary because the Ukrainian context will continue to be a factor of diplomatic crisis between East and West, to use Cold War terminology) thanks to diplomacy, the internal socio-political problems of Ukraine will not disappear. As for the Atlantic alliance, it is playing a big part in this crisis:

---

[22] Henry Kissinger, *Diplomacy*, Fayard, 1996, p. 123

if it gives in too much to Russian demands, its political power will be all the more contested and weakened. In 1948, Raymond Aron entitled the first chapter of one of his works *"Impossible peace, improbable war"*. [23] This is undoubtedly the formula that best describes the East-West rivalry, which has never ceased to grow and to be confirmed since the 2000s. Let us conclude this analysis with another thought of Raymond Aron's, the one presenting his realistic vision of international relations for which he evoked periods of peace and others of war. He had thus designated two essential actors: the soldier and the diplomat. This is the summary of the Ukrainian crisis. In this game, Vladimir Putin excels in both roles.

[23] Raymond Aron, *Le grand schisme*, Gallimard, 1948, 385 pp.

And Vladimir Putin gave the order to attack Ukraine...
February 2022

On the night of February 23 to 24, 2022, the scenario so feared in the West occurred: Russia launched a military operation in Ukraine. War was declared and condemned by the Western world. Vladimir Putin dared.

Immediately, the reactions were overwhelming.

Ukrainian President Volodymyr Zelensky has just declared martial law and is calling for Russian troops to suffer maximum losses. The European Union (EU) announced its intention to convene a crisis summit for February 24. British Prime Minister Boris Johnson called for an emergency meeting of NATO leaders. Vladimir Putin dared.

Media reports that explosions have been heard in Kiev, Odessa, and other major cities in Ukraine. The first military and civilian casualties are beginning to be counted in the dozens. The army announces territorial gains. Vladimir Putin has dared.

Eastern Europe is on fire for good. The Western world has never been upset like this by any external power since the end of the Cold War. Is the world order tipping over? Vladimir Putin has dared.

In the West, there is indignation, deploring, and condemnation. Certainly. Although the scenario of a war has been apprehended, it is now necessary to agree collectively on the response to be made. Should we attempt a new diplomatic operation of the last chance? In such a case, the master of the Kremlin will undoubtedly find himself in a position of strength. Should we respond to an armed attack by launching hostilities involving an international coalition? This would be the confirmation of a war between Russia and the Atlantic alliance. Vladimir Putin has shown his impatience and his fed up with communicating in return for negotiation conditions or the imposition of sanctions. He has unilaterally decided to put an end to his impatience. He does not have to take orders from anyone. The message sent is perfectly clear. He has prepared for war. We defend the hypothesis that he did not appreciate the dialogue with the Western actors, this way of setting conditions for him and threatening him if he does not respect them. Nothing is imposed on Russia. For the Atlantic alliance, it is astonishment. For the first time, a foreign power is provoking it to the point of carrying out its threats.

We are witnessing a pivotal moment in international relations. This is a certainty. We have always maintained that the scenario of a war was unlikely because the risks for the protagonists were great, considering the uncertainty that weighs on such a prospect. The Kremlin has shown its unwavering determination to go all the way and confront its Western adversaries, even if it means provoking a war. Our first reaction concerns the assurance of the Russian head of state. He feels strong enough to send his opponents to the ropes. In the previous days, he had repeatedly indicated that he was open to dialogue, while laying down conditions that suggested that he would not hesitate to go to the end of his thoughts. He thus left the door ajar to a diplomatic resolution of the crisis while communicating in a way that placed the Atlantic alliance in an uncomfortable position. After several days of incessant escalation of tensions, the master of the Kremlin has demonstrated once again that he is a formidable chess player. In other words, he has forced the issue. The ball is now in the Western camp. It is up to the latter to respond to force with force or to concede weakness in the face of a situation that is beyond its control. Moscow's message is: "I have assumed my choices. Do the same. "

By mid-day on February 24 in Western Europe, panic had taken hold of the financial markets. The stock markets were disrupted by the events that had occurred a few hours earlier in Eastern Europe. As for the oil markets, it was no surprise that prices soared. This was to be expected. Everyone is afraid of a war between Russia and NATO and all the disruptions that could be caused by such an event: a sudden increase in demand that supply could not meet, consequences on supplies, destruction of strategic infrastructure, etc. In such conditions, Brent crude oil was traded at over $105 per barrel while WTI was close to $100. These trading prices had not been reached since August 2014. At that time, the markets were coming out of a four-year long period with black gold trading prices above $100.

The Ukrainian crisis of 2013 and 2014 had influenced the exchange prices at the time, particularly due to the war in Donbass and the crisis in Crimea. These were already high since, as mentioned above, they were above $100 per barrel for almost four years. However, after the Ukrainian crisis in 2014, they began to fall. In February 2022, the story is different. Prices are inflamed as tensions take on a much more dramatic dimension with the "military operation" (dixit the official Kremlin communication) in Ukraine. The latter is officially being carried out to ensure peace in the separatist regions, recognized as independent by Moscow. There is a lot of uncertainty about NATO's reaction. In the West, the Russian intrusion into Ukrainian territory and the strikes carried out by Russia are perceived as a war. The latter pits Russia against Ukraine. However, this conflict would take on a different dimension if NATO, the United States, and the EU decided to join the fight.

There was no bluff. Vladimir Putin had set the tone, and he feels all the stronger for not condemning this military operation. The dramatic dimension is all the more critical as the Western world understands all the more that it is not only contested. It is being put to the test in a war of nerves for which it will have to make the right decision: either to calm the game and concede to Russia what it wants; or to engage in an economic conflict (the West will soon decide on new economic sanctions) or even an armed conflict that could lead to uncertain consequences for all. Russia has just shown that it will not back down from anything or anyone. Above all, it shows that it has succeeded in tipping the crisis into a scenario where it is now in a position of strength to negotiate. Despite threats, intimidation, and Western sanctions, it had warned that it would be open to dialogue as long as no quid pro quo was imposed. The Western alliance now has little time to counter the Russian offensive.

In Raymond Aron's vision of international relations, the soldier and the diplomat were the main characters. The soldier has just struck. Will another one strike back, or will the diplomat take over? We have never been so close to a war between Russia and the Atlantic alliance, although we thought that such a scenario was unlikely to happen. Diplomacy has not definitely failed. Hostilities can quickly stop, but in the Western camp, the reflection must focus on the following question: how to dialogue while not providing the impression that Russia is giving in to its demands? Like the attacks of September 11, 2001, which marked a turning point in contemporary international relations, the night of February 23-24, 2022, will certainly leave a mark on the evolution of international relations in the 21st century.

Western domination has never been so shaken since the end of the Cold War.

The Russian hybrid war
February 2022

On the night of February 23-24, 2022, the world was shocked when the Kremlin officially announced the launch of a military operation in the pro-Russian separatist areas of Ukraine. This decision was the next step towards Russian recognition of the independence of the Donetsk and Lugansk Republics. These recognitions were refuted by the Western world. How far was Vladimir Putin prepared to go to show his bellicose intentions and provoke those with whom dialogue remains complicated? The answer was not long in coming. Russian troops were quickly ordered to advance into Ukrainian territory and conduct military operations in several regions. Russia did not fail to announce its intention to take Kiev and to remove President Zelensky, who is rumored in the West to be Moscow's number one target. The Russian intervention in Ukraine is of great concern to the Western world. What does Vladimir Putin really want? Contrary to some ideas in the West, Russian nationalism is predominant in Russia. The Russians do not condemn the intervention in Ukraine. On the Western side, it is certain that the situation is presented in terms of lies, of manipulation orchestrated by the Russian leadership. In Moscow, the understanding of the problem is different. We are convinced that Vladimir Putin will have no choice but to win the war in order to stay in power. If he loses it, the stability of the political regime will be called into question. From then on, the Western camp is betting on internal destabilization: if the war in Ukraine lasts and generates many Russian victims, a protest movement could be born. In short, for Vladimir Putin, Ukraine must not become a new Afghanistan.

In the media, images of desolation quickly made the rounds. Civilian and military victims, buildings and other constructions hit by explosions, scenes of mass exodus of many Ukrainians, etc. are all evidence that a war has truly been unleashed in Eastern Europe... although Russia denies it. The latter maintains a vocabulary that the West does not accept when it evokes a military operation for peace purposes... Since then, cities have been besieged. Civilian and military victims are now counted in the hundreds or even thousands. Several large cities in the country are now like fields of ruins. The images are shocking. Russia has pushed the provocation to a point of no return. In Kiev and in the rest of the country, the armed opposition has organized itself and has the logistical support of several countries. The Russian offensive is encountering more consistent resistance than it could have imagined. In the media, a lot of information is circulating, some of which is sometimes contradictory. We try to understand how the Kremlin has set up this hybrid war. It is indeed an opposition that is materialized by an armed engagement in Ukraine but also by a real strategy concerning information. The problem is that when one sorts through the information that circulates, it is not easy to detect the good ones. In the West, it is said that Russia has underestimated the Ukrainian resistance, that the Russian armed forces are facing shortages of gasoline and food supplies, that some Russian battalions are now refusing to fight against a brotherly people, that the Russian army has been given false information about the real reasons for its presence near the Ukrainian borders for several weeks, etc. In sum, the Western world is beginning to defend the thesis that the Russian President has accumulated errors of judgment or assessment. There are also whispers that many movements rejecting the war are becoming more and more visible in Russia. It is certain that this war is not unanimously approved in the West. In the big Russian cities, there are certainly people who are opposed to the war, but there is no real popular vindication.

On the other hand, the turn of events is all the more worrying because at the beginning of March 2022, a new threat sent shivers down the spine of the world: Russian strikes hit Ukraine's largest nuclear power plant, Zaporizhzhia. These were obviously not accidental strikes. This nuclear infrastructure was well targeted. The determination of the Kremlin seems more formidable than ever. This is one more step towards the outbreak of a nuclear conflict. Yet, in the West, military, political and other analysts refuse to believe that Russia could "draw" nuclear weapons in this way. In short, the strikes on the Zaporizhzhia power plant are just another warning from Moscow, but one that is becoming increasingly worrying.

Moscow has a different view on the same topic. Who is telling the truth? Meanwhile, the Western world is multiplying economic sanctions against Moscow. The Western response to arms is not a desire to suffocate the Russian economy. Ukraine benefits from substantial logistical assistance from its allies. Similarly, the European Union (EU) is now studying Ukraine's, Georgia's, and Moldova's applications for membership. NATO is preparing for any eventuality. French President Emmanuel Macron maintains a regular dialogue with his Russian counterpart. Bilateral discussions between Ukraine and Russia are underway, but the demands of each party seem to be too far apart to expect a rapid easing of tensions. One solution being considered is the partition of Ukraine. We will come back to this, but we are not convinced that such an outcome would solve the country's problems.

Finally, how can we not mention the United States and China? Both remain rather discreet. Certainly, this armed opposition in Ukraine is taking place far from their borders. On the side of Washington, the discretion is all the more surprising as the United States is part of NATO. The apparent war of nerves, as described in another reflection in this book, is also taking place in the darkest recesses of the American political establishment. Ukraine is among the countries of greatest interest to the United States because this former Soviet republic is a key strategic area in Eastern Europe. We will come back to this later, but let's remember the events of Maidan in 2013 and the unwavering support given by the American leaders of the time, including Hillary Clinton who went there. There are obviously other interests that probably explain, in part, the American position today: it is observing, following the evolution of things, and is not particularly threatening towards Russia, except that it provides logistical support to Ukraine. Vladimir Putin has implemented what he calls a "military intervention" in Ukraine. Why didn't he do it with the Baltic countries or Finland? The countries mentioned are all part of the EU and NATO, except for Finland, which, in view of the Ukrainian crisis, quickly showed its willingness to join the Atlantic organization. An aggression against one of these countries would necessarily have led to a war involving many state actors. With Ukraine, this is not the case. Kiev has the political support of the Western world, but no one has so far intervened there to fight the Russian armed forces. The West believes that Vladimir Putin has an irrepressible desire for territorial conquest. There are some who argue that he will not stop at Ukraine. In such a case, this would obviously raise the question of starting a large-scale war... However, would this be his real ambition? The doubt is allowed. However, let's try to understand what the interests of this Ukrainian crisis are. In the West, everything related to the master of the Kremlin is now the subject of heated, acerbic, and depreciatory comments about his person. Everything that comes from Russia is suspect. In Russia, Western information is castigated as a form of anti-Russian propaganda. The information war has been going on for a long time. It is now accompanied by an armed struggle in

Ukraine between the Russian and Ukrainian armies. Russia is now relying on this armed struggle to pose new threats to the West, while the latter is intensifying its economic sanctions against Moscow. As for diplomatic dialogue, although it seems complex, it can still be the key to many compromises. On the other hand, the outcome of the Ukrainian crisis will have an impact on the course of international relations. Russia has made it clear that it intends to take on the West and show that it is a major political and military power. While Western leaders fear that this crisis will be long-lasting, it would be surprising if it were to end quickly...

Accusations on both sides: what objectivity?

In Russia and in the West, the Ukrainian crisis is not presented in the same way. In Russia, the official position is that the country was attacked by the Ukrainian army. In the West, the Russian military intervention is described as aggression and a declaration of war against Ukraine. In Russia, the economic sanctions imposed by the Western alliance are castigated. In the West, the irrationality and madness of the President of the Federation is denounced as endangering world security. On each side, the information about the Ukrainian crisis is presented differently. If there is one area in which Russia and the Western alliance agree, it is precisely the one that tends to assert that the opposing side is circulating false information. There is no point in denying it: there have been lies. When it was said that the Zaporizhzhia nuclear power plant had been hit by strikes, the Western world immediately said that the strikes were Russian. In Russia, the story was different. It was acknowledged that strikes had been carried out in this geographical area, but that the incidents at the nuclear power plant were not the fault of the Russian army. Who is telling the truth? There must be someone who is not telling the truth. This is just one example. There are many points of discrepancy between the versions given in Russia and in the West. For example, when the Western alliance claims that Russian troops in Ukraine are morally damaged by local resistance and that large-scale protests are taking place in Russia, Moscow, on the other hand, believes that the army is engaged in a military operation in which it believes, and that the morale of the troops is high. It is therefore difficult to assess the quality of the information that is circulating. Is it true? Are they exaggerated? From our point of view, we come back to an analysis that is not based solely on the apprehension of the information communicated, but rather on the lasting trends that have marked the difficult diplomatic relations between Russia and the Western world in recent years.

When we talk about a hybrid war, we must consider that the current Ukrainian crisis is unfortunately not surprising. It is occurring in a sensitive context in which the grounds for disagreement have continued to grow in intensity since then. It would be wrong to believe that the triggering element dates back to 2013. The origins are more distant. There were several gas crises between 2005 and 2009, to name but a few. They concerned the price and distribution of Russian natural gas transiting through Ukraine. There was a lull between 2010 and 2014. However, this period corresponded to the years of governance of Viktor Yanukovych, a member of a pro-Russian political party. It was following his decision to suspend the association agreement between Ukraine and the EU that a vast protest movement took hold of Kiev and the country's main cities. Similarly, it should be recalled that under President Trump in the United States, although Russia has always been in the crosshairs of Western forces, the New York businessman had calmed tensions with Moscow by naming Beijing as the main enemy of Washington. Is it necessary to recall that the Democratic camp has always tried to show suspicious links between Donald Trump and Russia? The moments in which the Ukrainian crisis was most intense occurred under Democratic rule in the United States.

The current crisis is undoubtedly more complex than it is presented in the media, although it is explained that Russia has been engaged in cyberattacks and disinformation campaigns for several years. The Western world is convinced that Russia has used many stratagems to influence the election campaign of the 2016 American presidential term. Russia has always denied and refuted these Western accusations, although they claim to be based on evidence. On the other hand, in NATO airspace, the vast majority of aircraft apprehended for flight irregularities are Russian. There are few cases of non-Russian aircraft getting lost in the airspace of the Atlantic alliance and not responding to calls from the requesting control towers.

Apart from the Ukrainian crisis, it is undeniable that things have happened that have fueled the difficult diplomatic relations between Russia and the Western alliance, be it NATO or the EU. On both sides, when it comes to the opponent, compliments are rare. Thus, political leaders and the media describe Russia and President Putin with unkind words. It goes without saying that the reciprocal is true on the Russian side. This state of affairs does not facilitate dialogue. The West is suspicious of Russia and vice versa. The escalation of tensions and threats orchestrated by President Putin have made the world shudder. How far is he prepared to go? When he mentions the possibility of using nuclear force, an old Cold War flavor resurfaces. The world had not been subjected to such a threat since the 1960s. Immediately, the reactions in the West were overwhelming: President Putin would have become uncontrollable and ready to do anything to achieve his goals, including the use of nuclear power! Of course, it is difficult to decipher his true intentions. It is disconcerting because he goes far in making threats and shows above all that he is ready to intensify their execution if he does not obtain the negotiation conditions he demands.

The military intervention in Ukraine is dramatic in many ways. The victims are numerous, both on the Ukrainian and Russian sides. There are obviously civilian victims. Some of the bombed cities look like fields of ruins. There is indeed an armed opposition between the Ukrainian and Russian forces. In Ukraine, many volunteers have joined the ranks of the armed resistance against the Russian occupiers. A foreign legion of non-Ukrainian fighters has come to assist in this opposition to Russia. In the eyes of the Western world, Moscow has committed the irreparable in unleashing the hostilities. In the Kremlin, it is said that the aggressor is Ukrainian. The arm-wrestling is engaged. While fighting in Ukraine, Russia defies the Atlantic alliance. The latter was initially content to respond with economic sanctions, the intensity of which increased with each new Russian threat or decision. The battle is not only armed and littered with bellicose intimidation. It is also fought at the level of information. This last one occupies a preponderant role, considering moreover the weight of social networks and the Internet for the quasi-instantaneous diffusion of information. This also contributes to the exacerbation of feelings. Within the Atlantic alliance, the decisions of President Putin are severely criticized. In Moscow and Kiev, for various reasons, nationalism is exacerbated. Once again, Russian citizens are expressing their disagreement or disapproval of the armed conflict in Ukraine. On the other hand, one should not underestimate the nationalist impulse that approves the operations being carried out there. However, as we shall see later, the longer the conflict goes on, the more likely it is that the support currently shown for the Kremlin will wane. In Ukraine, the Russian military provocation has generated a resistance movement that has joined the national armed forces. Many men have expressed their willingness to join the ranks of volunteers ready to defend the homeland. President Zelensky became a real warlord and several political and other personalities decided to oppose the Russian forces on the ground. We can mention the former President Petro Poroshenko, the former boxer and mayor of Kiev Vitali Klitschko or the former soccer player Oleg Luzhny. According to the videos circulating on the Internet and other information, some of which are authentic and others probably more questionable, we have reached a turning point in the crisis since the Russians and the Ukrainians who are fighting are each animated by a nationalist feeling. On the Western side, the difficulties encountered by the Russian troops are regularly mentioned. In Russia, on the contrary, they assure that the operations are progressing positively. The truth is that information is one of the major issues in this crisis, as in all other crises, but the technological means are now such that it is possible to disseminate large flows of information, founded or unfounded, in a minimum of time. A well-targeted information campaign generally does not leave the recipient of the message unmoved.

Western fears vs. Russian determination

Since President Putin brandished the nuclear threat, the world has been reminded of the darkest hours of the Cuban missile crisis when it held its breath at the determination shown by John Fitzgerald Kennedy and Nikita Khrushchev. This threat has been repeated several times since February 27 and one would almost forget that the Russian army had taken control of the Chernobyl nuclear power plant two days earlier. Nuclear provocation is the ultimate threat. It is the last resort when dialogue seems impossible. Yet a nuclear threat must be analyzed carefully. It does not necessarily indicate a move to action, quite the contrary.

In the middle of March 2022, the Western media are looking into the state of President Putin's mental health. They do not fail to question specialists in international relations or doctors and other specialists of the mind. Some believe that the master of the Kremlin is suffering from Hubris syndrome. Psychoanalysts refer to this syndrome as a narcissistic, arrogant, pretentious, lying, manipulative or glory-seeking person. For some, the main fear weighing on the person of Vladimir Putin is a fierce desire to show that he is the master of the game and that therefore, he dictates the rules, even if it means brandishing the most extreme eventualities. By letting a nuclear threat hover, he has succeeded in his communication operation: he has expressed what the whole world fears. As soon as the use of a nuclear weapon is mentioned, it is as if everyone is holding their breath. It is certain that Russia has nuclear weapons powerful enough to cause irreversible damage on a global scale. But is this what Vladimir Putin wants? Would he be ready for such an extreme?

It is difficult to have a categorical opinion on the matter because the Russian number one knows how to be scathing in his statements. He is certainly intimidating. According to people who have known him, he does not appreciate contradiction. The problem lies in the credibility of such a threat. It should not be underestimated. However, the bluff option should not be ruled out. Vladimir Putin's strength has been to communicate with sufficient gravity, solemnity, and determination that any recipient of the message must understand that he will not hesitate to use nuclear force if he deems it necessary. As soon as he invoked this possibility, the opposing critics went up a notch: President Putin had become crazy, uncontrollable, unmanageable, and dangerous in many ways. Weapons and conflict specialists see the nuclear threat differently. For them, when it is brandished in such circumstances, it should be understood that it will not be carried out because the author of the threat knows that if it is carried out, the adversary will immediately retaliate in kind. When he threatens with nuclear weapons, he is not attacking Ukraine but NATO, which also has nuclear weapons. If he remained a pragmatic statesman, why would he carry out a threat for which he would surely suffer damaging consequences for his country? Of course, this reasoning no longer holds if he is determined to use nuclear weapons, as those who see him as suffering from Hubris syndrome fear. In the meantime, everyone is forming an opinion on the matter without having any certainty. It is all speculation in terms of interpretation.

On the other hand, if there is one proven fact, it is that of the threat made by Vladimir Putin. He leaves the Western camp to ponder the degree of credibility of the threat. In short, the more unpredictable he is perceived to be, the more he is satisfied. Like a game of chess, he hopes to confuse those he is addressing. Some say that he is simply applying what he was taught in the KGB [24] ; beyond this assumption, he blows hot and cold all the time. He acts, executes what he "promised" to do, but is always open to dialogue. The problem is that the bond of trust has been consumed with his Western interlocutors, who see him as a liar, a manipulator and a person blinded by disproportionate ambitions that are dangerous for world security. Some people are now saying that he does not want to limit himself to an invasion of Ukraine... Vladimir Putin has succeeded in

---

[24] Author's note: КГБ, Комитет государственной безопасности, literally the Committee for State Security, an intelligence service created in the Soviet era.

sowing confusion in the Western camp. By confusion, one must understand that no one is able to state with certainty what he really intends to do or decide. But he shows the face of a man who is determined to get what he wants at any cost. The Atlantic alliance is supporting Ukraine with logistical assistance, much to the chagrin of President Zelensky, who would appreciate more than just material assistance. The war is between Russia and Ukraine, but NATO would only intervene as a last resort.

In the meantime, the EU and the US have continued to increase the intensity of economic sanctions against Russia and many Russian citizens, both oligarchs and politicians. The exclusion of Russian banks from the SWIFT platform has been detrimental in the sense that the ruble has rapidly declined against the dollar. Russia is therefore exposed to the risk of high inflation. It is rumored that in a short time the country could find itself in default of payments, that is to say that it could no longer honor its financial commitments in time with its creditors. On March 8, 2022, the United States declared an embargo on Russian oil. [25] Clearly, the United States will no longer import Russian black gold until further notice. This sanction may lead to others. The United Kingdom quickly expressed its willingness to do the same. The share of Russian oil in US consumption is very much in the minority, but the European allies could be moving towards a similar decision... although it needs to be further matured before being enacted because within the EU, hydrocarbon needs are partly met by Russia. [26] In the absence of a ban on Russian hydrocarbon imports, the European Commission is initially recommending that member states diversify their sources of

---

[25] Véronique Le Billon, *"Ukraine : les Etats-Unis lancent un embargo sur le pétrole russe"*, www.lesechos.fr, March 8, 2022
[26] *"Gaz russe : faute d'embargo, l'UE veut réduire de deux tiers ses importations"*, www.lefigaro.fr, March 8, 2022

supply. A few hours later, the official voice of the Kremlin warned that any sanctions against Russia would have negative effects for the punishers, since a sharp rise in food prices would be expected.

In Europe, the Ukrainian crisis is not perceived in the same way as in the United States. The reason is simple: it is happening on the doorstep of the EU. Moreover, the politician who is trying to maintain dialogue with Moscow is none other than President Macron. The latter has shown a remarkable attitude because, although shaken by the determination of his Russian alter ego to be in a position of strength at the negotiating table, he is now the embodiment of the Western political authority that does not intend to relax its efforts to work for diplomacy, while he wants to be intransigent to negotiate with Moscow. The Western camp needs a representative who keeps in touch with President Putin. The great difficulty for the Western camp is precisely not to fall into the trap of Russian provocation. War is a different response. It is certain that the Atlanticist world cannot remain without reaction to the military operation led by the Kremlin in Ukraine, but two weeks after the beginning of hostilities, although NATO is now ready to intervene if necessary, a confrontation between Russia and the Atlantic alliance is not topical. In view of the number of countries that would then be involved in armed confrontation, we could be talking about a world war. It is not certain that this is what Russia wants. The Western world is increasing its economic pressure on Moscow but does not intend to engage in an armed conflict. In this case, the longer the war lasts in Ukraine, the more it will weaken Russia.

The long war, the main enemy of Russia
Once again, it all depends on who is announcing the message: when it is the West, it defends the idea that a long

war in Ukraine will be detrimental to the economy and political stability of the Russian regime. In Russia, the scenario of a long military intervention in the Ukrainian neighbor is excluded: the outcome will be quick and victorious. Russia will come out of it stronger. For several weeks now, the whole of the European continent has been shaken by this crisis, which is becoming increasingly intense in its Eastern part. In the Western media, it is often said that Vladimir Putin has made several errors of judgement in intervening in Ukraine. Firstly, by doing so, he has strengthened cohesion within the EU but also within NATO. Second, he has energized the nationalism that animates many Ukrainian volunteers who are ready to take up arms to defend their homeland against the Russian invader. Third, images have circulated showing an endless column of Russian military vehicles at a standstill on their way to Kiev. This column is said to stretch for sixty kilometers. According to the media, the Russian army is facing fuel and food shortages.

Similarly, the power of images can have an impact in Russia, which has protected itself against certain risks by cutting off access to websites and social networks. The Ukrainian army has broadcast images of Russian soldiers taken prisoner. This practice has been denounced as a violation of international law, notably by the Red Cross. The Ukrainian army intended to exert psychological pressure on Russia by broadcasting images of young men captured in combat who testify against the Kremlin's decision to have invaded Ukrainian territory. Some people say that Moscow lied to them. They were not told the truth. They were not told the real purpose of the maneuver when the troops were deployed on the Ukrainian border a few weeks earlier. The same would have happened when the order was given to enter Ukraine, first in the territories recognized by Russia as independent and sovereign. This communication strategy is not insignificant because the mothers of the military represent a powerful "lobby" in Russia. [27] Moreover, the Ukrainians have gone so far as to create a website so that any mother of a Russian soldier sent to Ukraine can find out whether her son is still alive or not, since the names of the killed and slaughtered combatants are announced there. This is the kind of tool that can work against the Kremlin in the event of a prolonged conflict. In such a case, the Kremlin would be blamed for bringing many dead back to Russia. At the end of February 2022, Kiev declared that Russian losses amounted to four thousand three hundred men, while politician Lev Shlossberg put forward the idea that the Russian army was moving with mobile crematoriums to be able to quickly burn the bodies of killed Russian soldiers so as not to leave any traces. [28] On March 10, 2022, the Western media relayed new information that shocked the West: The Russian army had carried out strikes on a maternity hospital in Mariupol. Russia confirmed the facts but justified them by saying that this building was a fallback base for Ukrainian nationalists. The next morning, President Zelensky announced that a humanitarian corridor which had been set up for the evacuation of civilians had in turn been attacked by the Russian army. This humanitarian corridor was supposed to allow the inhabitants of the cities of Mariupol and Volnovakha to leave the area.

---

[27] Author's note: The Union of Committees of Soldiers' Mothers of Russia (Russian: Союз комитетов солдатских матерей России). It is a non-governmental organization established in 1989, the year that marked the end of the Soviet military intervention in Afghanistan. Its influence has been growing in Russian civil life ever since. It seeks to help young people who must perform their military service, to make their rights known and respected. Since its creation, Russia has been involved in several deadly wars, especially in the Caucasus.

[28] *"Guerre en Ukraine : un site internet pour retrouver les soldats russes tués"*, www.cnews.fr, February 27, 2022

Every day, new facts are published and shock public opinion, whether it is Western or Russian, because it is certain, as already mentioned, that the presentation of information is not the same depending on whether one is in Russia or the West. In both camps, "positive" information is conveyed. On the Russian side, they report progress on Ukrainian territory and the destruction of a good number of strategic infrastructures. On the other side, they are communicating in a different way, stating that the Russian troops are encountering difficulties for which they were not prepared, and that the morale of the troops has been affected. On both sides, real information is circulating. A lot of infrastructural destruction has been reported. As for the fighting, the local resistance is undoubtedly more consistent than what could have been apprehended by Moscow. In this case, it is on this point that the Atlantic alliance is now betting: to ensure that the Russian army is engaged in a long-term conflict in Ukraine so that the destabilization in Russia comes from inside. In other words, like the conflicts that characterized the Cold War in the past, the great military powers do not confront each other directly. When one of them engages in the field, the other responds with economic and logistical support. This is what is happening with Ukraine, which is receiving economic and material aid to organize the armed struggle against Russia, but with the exception of foreign volunteers who have decided to come and lend a hand to Ukrainian fighters, no country in the Atlantic alliance has sent troops to fight against Russia.

The Western world has a coherent discourse when it wants to show its firmness towards Russia while announcing that it wants to favor diplomacy over war. This is precisely what is being put in place. It is not closing the door to a dialogue with Vladimir Putin, although the latter has undoubtedly reduced his capital of good faith in the eyes of the West. On the other hand, the economic sanctions, which aim to reach the Russian economic system as quickly as possible, are in reality complementary weapons to the armed struggle proposed by the Ukrainian troops and their voluntary supporters. In Kiev, the perception of the situation is different. President Zelensky regrets that the allied commitment is not more "advanced". In other words, he is asking his supporters to send troops ready to fight. This request is not currently on NATO's agenda. The strategy is clear. There will be no armed intervention against Russia unless it does the irreparable by attacking an EU or NATO member jurisdiction... or by carrying out its nuclear threat. If the Ukrainian resistance proves to be valiant and above all resistant, considering the arsenal of economic sanctions against Russia, the chances are indeed high of witnessing a prolonged armed conflict that would constitute a risk of political and social destabilization for the Kremlin. On the one hand, we have referred to this committee of Russian soldiers' mothers. Its power of influence in Russia should not be underestimated. A movement started by angry mothers can quickly spread nationwide. The longer the war goes on, the greater the losses. That is why the authorities spoke of a military operation for security purposes that had to be quick rather than talk of war. On the other hand, many Russian personalities, including the famous oligarchs, find themselves personally sanctioned by the Western world. The case of Roman Abramovich has been widely publicized. The businessman is the owner of the London soccer club Chelsea. With the outbreak of hostilities, he returned to Russia and quickly made known his intention to sell the club. Several buyers expressed interest. However, the sale process was simply suspended. Roman Abramovich is one of the people subject to Western sanctions. His case is not isolated. That is why the Western world is also banking on the strategy of freezing the bank and other assets of these businessmen, so that they will finally become annoyed and advocate for interests that differ from those of the Kremlin.

In sum, before and after the outbreak of hostilities, President Putin waged a war of nerves with Ukraine and the Atlantic alliance. Since then, if Ukraine has responded to these provocations with arms because of the presence of the Russian army on its territory, the Kremlin would undoubtedly have wished for a different reaction from Kiev's Western allies. Faced with Russian military hard power, the West responds with economic soft power. The latter does not respond to Moscow's provocations as the Russian capital would have liked. The West is thwarting Russia's plans. For the strategy of the Atlantic alliance to have any chance of achieving the desired objectives, there is one insurmountable condition: the conflict in Ukraine must be prolonged. If the Russian army cannot be defeated, the core of the Western commitment is to reach the Russian economy, but also the national public opinion and the business circles that might disagree with the official positions of the Kremlin. When Russia announced the launch of its military intervention on the night of 23 to 24 February 2022, we were surprised by the Western reaction, which seemed to betray an unpreparedness for this scenario. However, many analysts expected a Russian incursion into Ukraine. On February 24, the trend in Europe was to call emergency meetings within the EU and NATO. Two weeks after Vladimir Putin's order to conduct a large-scale military mission, the Western response is clear: while the master of the Kremlin is seeking Ukrainian capitulation, his Western adversaries are aiming at the same goal in Moscow but with a very different strategy.

The "surprising" withdrawal of the United States and China
On March 10, 2022, while diplomatic talks were being held in Antalya, Turkey, Ukraine's Foreign Minister

said he had not found common ground for a ceasefire with his Russian counterpart. The next day, NATO Secretary General Jens Stoltenberg announced that the Atlantic alliance did not want to engage in an open war with Russia. The same day, an EU Council was held in Versailles, France, to discuss, among other things, the question of Ukrainian membership in the organization, which includes twenty-seven member states. In the media, even before the event, one idea stands out: Ukraine will not join the EU in the short term. One of the arguments is that this collegial organization does not allow countries at war to join. All this only confirms that the war is between Ukraine and Russia, that Ukraine has the strong support of the Western world, but that the latter's entry into the war is not in the cards. For Ukraine, all this means that it must either continue the war effort against the Russian army or surrender. Meanwhile, Russia seems more determined than ever to make no concessions to Kiev's diplomacy. While the crisis is escalating in Europe, the United States and China are communicating little on the topic.

It would be a lie to say that Washington is not concerned about the situation. First, the United States is a member of NATO. In other words, if the war were to end up pitting the Atlantic organization against Russia, Uncle Sam's country would therefore be directly involved in the conflict. The White House's apprehension of this crisis confirms the position of its European partners: economic sanctions are validated, and logistical support has been put in place to help the Ukrainian armed forces. President Biden's position was quickly made clear when he stated that he was ready to intervene militarily if a NATO territory was the object of armed Russian attacks; however, he ruled out a military operation in Ukraine. In the United States and in Europe, everyone is on the same wavelength as to the strategy to adopt to counter Russian interests. The convergences concern the substance. It is on the form that there are divergences. We have already mentioned the embargo decided by Washington on Russian hydrocarbon imports. In this respect, the United States is more assertive than the EU, but this can be explained by the fact that Russian oil accounts for a very large minority of American consumption. Clearly, the United States can easily do without Russian oil for its domestic needs. This is not the case for the EU. Although the EU is now firmly focused on a strategy of diversifying its suppliers to be less dependent on Russian hydrocarbon imports, it is not possible to suddenly impose an embargo without having secured other sources of supply.

Joe Biden must consider several issues for which he knows he is expected to act both on the national and international scene. He is keeping in mind that a bad decision will be detrimental to him a few months before the mid-term elections, which could then see Americans vote favorably for Republican candidates for the House of Representatives and Senate. This is probably why he is cautious about Russian provocations. He must stand firm in the eyes of his constituents. He cannot show any sign of weakness in the face of a leader who hammers out a virile communication to his opponents. On the other hand, while he refuses to concede anything to Vladimir Putin, he does not neglect China. Indeed, while the Ukrainian crisis is monopolizing most of the media attention, it is not to be excluded that Vladimir Putin's determination has not given Beijing some ideas. We come back to this: the Ukrainian crisis is very revealing of this reality of international relations within which Western domination is now more than ever contested. Russia has taken the plunge by daring to provoke the Atlantic alliance with what it calls a "demilitarization" and "denazification" operation in Ukraine. Such Russian justifications were unacceptable to the West. Since then, the Kremlin has been pursuing a communication of legitimization of all decisions taken for the military intervention in Ukraine. Within the Atlantic alliance, the Russian arguments are perceived as an escalation of provocation aimed at testing the "tolerance threshold" of the latter, even to the point of including a nuclear threat. However, it is certain that Russia has disturbed the international order. Since Vladimir Putin took over as president, it has been involved in several wars. This time, by attacking Ukraine, he is also targeting all the countries that support Kiev. From this point of view, he is disturbing international relations more than ever, while the great contemporary duel is between the United States and China.

Beijing's position is interesting because it is rather discreet. The official word on the Ukrainian crisis is rather rare. It is not non-existent for all that. It wants to be cautious. Officially, China did not support the Russian offensive in Ukraine, nor did it condemn it. Xi Jinping and Vladimir Putin are said to share excellent friendly relations. Considering the rather complicated and tumultuous past relations between the two countries, the two statesmen certainly appreciate each other but are moving forward carefully. They both show pragmatism. When the interests of both countries converge, they know how to get along. Thus, three weeks before the launch of Russian military operations in Ukraine, they had jointly communicated their reticence regarding the expansionist ambitions of NATO in Europe and the Aukus in the Indo-Pacific region. In the West, this announcement sounded like a serious warning. It was seen as a dangerous alliance while Russian troops had been massed for several weeks near Ukraine. The fact that China joined in this declaration was even more worrying given the West's belief that it might have bellicose ambitions towards Taiwan. Moreover, in the preceding months, the two countries had also communicated about the high-tech weapons that both had managed to develop. Clearly, when the Kremlin decided to intervene in Ukraine, a chill ran through Europe and North America: would Moscow not have given Beijing ideas in the China Sea? This is a threat that is taken into consideration by the United States. However, President Xi Jinping is not known for engaging his country in wars as his Russian counterpart may be. In view of the evolution of international relations, we cannot blame the Western world for being suspicious of China.

Possible partition, unsolvable national ills

Discussions between Ukraine and Russia are taking place regularly. This is a clear sign that the dialogue is not broken. However, the wishes expressed by the two countries are far apart. This augurs a lasting Ukrainian crisis... unless one of the belligerents capitulates and expresses the will to stop this war. The Ukrainian resistance has organized itself and is receiving Western aid. In mid-March 2022, the United States and then several European states released funds to Kiev. Until now, there was no question of NATO member countries getting involved in any other way. The support does not include the intervention of soldiers against the Russian armed forces. This position irritates President Zelensky, who does not hesitate to express it openly. After all, the Western world assures him of its unwavering support... but to a certain extent. In Russia, they are still counting on a quick victory, which is however slow to emerge. In the West, it is said that the Russian tactics are encountering many difficulties and that the Ukrainian resistance is strongly opposing the Kremlin's plans. In the meantime, sanctions continue to pile up against Russia.

On March 15, the U.S. Senate passed a resolution designating Vladimir Putin as a "war criminal. The next day, President Biden, in turn, gave the same designation to his Russian alter ego. This designation was taken up in the wake by several European heads of state and government. This accusation is not insignificant. President Putin sees the pressure on him increasing. One does not accuse someone of war crimes without reason. Clearly, a new threat hangs over him: he is now exposed to legal proceedings. In other words, he will have no choice but to win the war and isolate himself on the international scene in order to escape criminal prosecution. This means that all means will be used to weaken him further. This reinforces our idea that the longer the war goes on, the more Vladimir Putin will be exposed to the risks of internal destabilization in Russia. In short, the vice is tightening for Russia and the man who presides over it: if he expects to remain the unmovable number one, the consequence will be an even longer isolation of the country on the international scene.

The involvement of many Ukrainian personalities in the conflict confirms the nationalist impetus that has seized the country to fight the invader. The determination of the Ukrainian resistance is such that it seems unthinkable that the leaders in Kiev could accept a scenario of capitulation and thus allow Russia to install a pro-Russian leader at the head of the country. Several hypotheses can be envisaged, but all will come up against the fierce will of the Ukrainian nation to defend its territory. In this sense, this is what makes us think that this war will last a long time. On March 20, a message from Turkey, the country where Russian and Ukrainian officials meet, suggested that an agreement could soon be reached between the enemy brothers. Such communication is hopeful. However, the fighting continues in several regions of Ukraine while the army is struggling to advance as it would like. As already indicated, it is unlikely that President Putin will back down. He is engaged in a war and does not expect to come out a loser. In short, this is tantamount to saying that if an agreement were to be negotiated, it would be disadvantageous for Kiev... but the Ukrainian capital never stops reminding us that it does not intend to give up its arms.

Let us not forget the hypothesis of an agreement leading to the partition of Ukraine. We do not believe in this scenario because President Zelensky certainly does not intend to do Russia any favors. However, if this hypothesis were to be considered, the partition of the country would not solve the national problems because if some regions are indeed inhabited by a pro-Ukrainian or pro-Russian majority, others are much more mixed. It goes without saying that many people, whether they feel Ukrainian or Russian, condemn the fighting. Many consider the incongruity of such a war between brotherly peoples. This war is not the result of a poisonous animosity between these peoples, but rather the decision of one man determined to impose his will on others. The problem is that on the Ukrainian side, misunderstanding quickly gave way to a fierce determination to fight the enemy. This armed opposition will leave a visible scar for a long time that will be difficult to erase. From then on, it will be difficult to envisage a cohabitation between pro-Kiev and pro-Moscow militants in Ukraine. The war will have passed by and exacerbated feelings. In other words, if a partition of the country is technically possible, it will never forget the reasons that pushed its inhabitants to take up arms to fight the Russian army. Ukraine will remain a country where two nations coexist, but this cohabitation is made all the more difficult by the political positions and choices that led to this fratricidal war.

Conclusion

Like all armed conflicts, the war in Ukraine does not escape this endless truth that it is littered with horrors. Civilian victims are numerous. Families are separated. Many are torn apart because some members live in Russia and others in Ukraine. In the West, the Kremlin is castigated for having intentionally triggered military operations that it wishes to be brief and effective. The scenario is not going as planned. The Russian intrusion and the initial fighting fueled nationalist sentiment in Kiev. The men took up arms to defend the fatherland. President Zelensky set himself up as a symbol of resistance. He stayed in the country and exchanged the suit for the combat fatigues. He vowed to fight valiantly and defeat the enemy.

On the Russian side, they probably did not expect such a difficult armed struggle. The troops are advancing with difficulty and after a month of conflict, the Russian presence in Ukraine covers only a small part of the national territory. Russia is shelling many cities with heavy artillery. Some are destroyed. Some events make the headlines, especially when strikes hit hospitals, schools, or maternity wards. The Western world now accuses Vladimir Putin of war crimes. As for the Russian army, the Kremlin communicates in the sense of a constant mobilization and a justified intervention in Ukraine. On the Western side, the difficulties encountered on the ground, the numerous victims, the desertions, and the morale of the troops which does not seem to be in good shape are mentioned. In short, the war is taking place in conditions that were not foreseen by Moscow. Protest movements were organized in the country. Russian voices denounced the absurdity of attacking a brotherly people. President Putin is obliged to communicate to legitimize this military presence in Ukraine... and to call to order the oligarchs to support the war effort. The latter have been heavily sanctioned by the

Western world. Real estate and personal property have been seized, bank accounts have been frozen, and some are beginning to doubt the assurances of military victory promised by the Kremlin. If some remain silent, all share the same fear: losing everything.

Losing everything is what the Kremlin leadership is also exposed to. Despite the communication campaigns of disinformation, one must observe the situation with lucidity: one does not attack a territory of six hundred thousand square kilometers with two hundred thousand men. When Russia appeals to China for logistical and financial support, this request is questionable. The obvious deduction is that the situation was underestimated. President Putin was undoubtedly convinced that the war would be quick and that the overthrow of President Zelensky would take place quickly. Beyond facing fierce resistance, war is expensive. This is probably why he went so far as to threaten nuclear war. However, until proven otherwise, Russia is not at war with NATO, but with a country that is certainly supported financially and logistically by the member states of the Atlantic alliance and by the EU. The escalation of the nature of the threats suggests that Russia is getting annoyed with the course of operations with unexpected results. After a month of fighting, Russia has not won. On the contrary, it is weakened.

The Western world has taken the time to think about sanctioning Moscow. These sanctions are not only intended to suffocate the Russian economy but also to destabilize the country from inside. The longer the war in Ukraine goes on, the greater the chances that the country's calm will be disrupted by protests. Economic hardship and popular discontent can quickly become new enemies for the Kremlin. Considering all that has happened since the outbreak of hostilities, President Putin's room for maneuver is now very limited: he knows that if he fails in imposing himself in Ukraine, he will be challenged in Russia and the Western world will do its utmost to have him removed from power. In other words, to secure his power base, he has no choice but to win the war he has started and to succeed in overthrowing the Ukrainian government to place a new pro-Russian leader in Kiev... who would naturally be disavowed by the Western world.

While Ukrainians and Russians are trying to reach a diplomatic agreement in Turkey, the conditions on both sides seem too opposite for the conflict to end. The damage is too deep to imagine a cessation of hostilities in the light of what is happening. The Ukrainians are driven by a devouring desire to "hit the Russian". As for the Russians, it would be difficult to understand a halt to the fighting if they fail in imposing their conditions during negotiations with Ukraine. President Putin is playing for keeps. He has no other option than to win the war and impose his conditions... which will probably not be accepted by NATO because we suspect that in such a case, they would be unfavorable to the Atlantic alliance. Moreover, let us not make any predictions; other aspects of the crisis are of concern. We are witnessing an obvious problem of communication between the main political powers of the planet.

On March 19, a two-hour meeting allowed Joe Biden and Xi Jinping to exchange views on the Ukrainian crisis. The American leader warned his Chinese alter ego about the "consequences" that would hit China if it gave aid to Russia... Beijing continues to play with the West, blowing hot and cold. China has offered humanitarian aid to Ukraine but has never condemned Russia's military intervention. During the meeting with Joe Biden, Xi Jinping never characterized the situation by the word "war". China is therefore being evasive but does not intend to give in to American threats. International relations are changing at a rapid pace. The Sino-American rivalry can be seen in the way the two economic giants communicate and observe the hostilities in Ukraine. President Biden's communication is not the timeliest. The way he is signaling consequences for aid to Russia is inappropriate. This is not the way to communicate with China. The latter will not fail to indicate that it does not have to take orders from anyone. Thus, it leaves the suspense hanging. Will it help Russia? It will give itself time to reflect and make the Western world think about its hypothetical intentions. In this game, Xi Jinping will not hesitate to show that he is a remarkable strategist in matters of war of nerves.

In the West, Vladimir Putin's war is seen as a strategic mistake in the sense that he acted in this way to take advantage of the dissension within the EU and NATO as well as the internal ills that are undermining the United States. Since then, it has been whispered that the Russian President has promoted the existence of a new cohesion in Europe as well as within the Atlantic alliance. Why not? Some analyses point in this direction, but this is not the subject of our reflection. What interests us more is the communication deployed by the American authorities. For the time being, we are concerned by it.

In the arcane of international politics, it is sometimes difficult to advocate a resolutely firm discourse without encroaching on the terrain of threat. The exercise is difficult. President Biden has constantly reiterated his intention to remain firm towards Russia and China. Is it necessary to recall that American leadership is no longer as dominant as in the past? Moscow and Beijing no longer intend to be intimidated by Washington's rhetoric. In other words, when the United States ventures into the thinly veiled terrain of threat, the Chinese and Russian leaders do not intend to be impressed. On the contrary, they are showing with authority that Western injunctions will not prevent them from carrying out what they intend to do. The military operation decided by Vladimir Putin came a few days after an umpteenth attempt at dialogue by Emmanuel Macron, who had sounded out his Russian counterpart for the holding of an extraordinary summit on the Ukrainian crisis. The idea was to have Vladimir Putin and Joe Biden sit at the same table. The Russian head of state accepted the proposal in principle. In the wake of this, President Macron contacted his American alter ego. The latter responded favorably but set a condition: no summit in the event of an invasion of Ukraine by Russian troops. No one knows how this condition was perceived by Vladimir Putin, but it certainly influenced his decision to intervene in Ukraine. The fact of having imposed a condition undoubtedly displeased Moscow. This does not legitimize the military intervention. Moreover, it was probably planned, whether Joe Biden imposed a condition or not. On the other hand, we are convinced that his response to Emmanuel Macron's proposal was not the right one.

Our thinking is the same for the March 19 meeting between Joe Biden and Xi Jinping. Certainly, the United States must not show any form of weakness in the face of adversity. However, it must deal with an international reality in which there are actors who now intend to assert their military and / or economic hard power, as if to remind the White House that it is no longer the ultra-dominant leader of the past. To put it another way, the discourse that the United States was able to convey to the world when it ruled the world unchallenged is no longer relevant. Russia and China are communicating in this sense. It is imperative that the United States adapts its communication to the international reality. Joe Biden has made mistakes with

Vladimir Putin and Xi Jinping. He will not obtain anything by being threatening. As for the war in Ukraine, he can weaken Russia by supporting intensive economic pressure. On the other hand, regarding the "consequences" mentioned during his meeting with Xi Jinping, it is not certain that he has succeeded in dissuading his Chinese counterpart from anything. China wants to be discreet by choice. Nothing and no one will be able to take a threat seriously today if it feels able to retaliate as it sees fit if necessary.

Our opinion will undoubtedly not be unanimous. We assume it. Our respective professional experiences indicate that the Western discourse is no longer perceived in the same way in the world as it was in the past, notably during the period of post-Cold War ultra-domination until the tragic events of September 11, 2001. Since the Western world embarked on wars against international Islamist terrorism, there have been attitudes and communications that have displeased and shocked the international community. The weight of words is of paramount importance in international relations. When the Western world defends democratic values and justifies its interventions in the fight against terrorism, we must be concerned about how the recipients will understand the messages. This has already been seen with countries that have expressed their resentment at being equated with systems that espouse anti-democratic values and show leniency or more towards terrorist organizations while fighting against them. Poor communication cannot promote peace between peoples. It can, however, strain diplomatic relations.

In conclusion, when we talk about Samuel Huntington's thesis on the clash of civilizations, we add a communication dimension that seems unsurpassable. This thesis was written in the 1990s, when American ultra-domination was at its peak. Today, we still believe in this civilizational clash, considering that the United States is facing an adversary that no longer hides its ambitions and that has power arguments that induce a change in the way it communicates. Since the beginning of the 21st century, the world has changed considerably. Diplomacy must adapt to this reality. If it is understandable that the Western world seeks to remain dominant on the international scene, the way of communicating must consider the adversity that currently challenges its leadership in terms of hard power.

Vladimir Putin the irrational?
February 2022

The Russian-led military operation, to use the Kremlin's official terminology, has been strongly criticized in the West. The Atlantic alliance went through different emotions. Dismay, anger, desolation, and many others animated the debates that took place on February 24, 2022, in the European Union (EU), NATO and the White House. Everyone is criticizing Russian aggression, Moscow's clear desire to fight on military grounds, and the growing provocation that is leading to the path of war. Although the Kremlin defends itself by firing missiles and advancing armored troops into Ukrainian territory, these are acts of war. Everything happened so fast that the next day, European intelligence services announced that Russian armed forces were getting dangerously close to Kiev... For the Ukrainian capital, it is indeed feared that there will be a political overthrow and that President Zelensky will be forced to flee. In the West, the wave of indignation caused by the Russian offensive has been accompanied by very sharp comments against Vladimir Putin. Many describe him as a dangerous leader. Some have called him paranoid or irrational. It is understood that in view of the situation, while many did not rule out the risk of a war with Ukraine, all secretly hoped that the President would not carry out his threats.

In the Western camp, the tone is unanimous: Vladimir Putin has crossed the white line. He has gone too far in his provocation. In the media, emotions are running high. This man, for whom many recall his career in the KGB, constitutes the greatest threat to peace and security in Europe since the end of the Second World War. Former French Foreign Minister Hubert Védrine did not fail to show his anger by declaring that Vladimir Putin was undoubtedly a tactician but not a strategist. [29]

On February 25, at midday, Russia said it was open to negotiation... while setting the condition that Ukraine lay down its arms. The day before, the EU announced that it wanted to strengthen its sanctions against Moscow to an unprecedented level. As for the official communication of Joe Biden, it claimed to defend any piece of territory that is a member of NATO but did not consider sending troops to Ukraine... In other words, it must be understood that the Western alliance does not want to fight Russia head on. In other words, the Western alliance does not want to fight Russia head-on. Moreover, this only goes in the direction of the head of the German army who denounced his country's unpreparedness for war. [30]

For a long time, Russia has been suspected. It is often demonized. As for Vladimir Putin, the West often reproaches him for his authoritarianism, his icy and bellicose vision of international relations. Since he became the country's strongman, he is on his sixth military intervention of this kind. The Western media is quick to point out the disapproval of many Russians for invading Ukraine in this way. This may be the case. The military operation carried out by Moscow is certainly not unanimously approved in Russia. However, we do not share the view that Vladimir Putin has become irrational. On the contrary, we defend the idea that he is rational, that he is a fine tactician and strategist. Moreover, it is not incompatible to have these two qualities and to know defeat. He knows what he is doing, no doubt with a certain degree of lack of

---

[29] Eugénie Bastié, *"Hubert Védrine: "Poutine commet une erreur historique""*, www.lefigaro.fr, February 24, 2022
[30] *"Allemagne: Le chef de l'armée critique l'impréparation militaire du pays"*, www.challenges.fr, February 24, 2022

control over the situation if NATO ever decides to retaliate by force. The Western alliance seems to prefer other avenues of response than armed confrontation, for which it hopes to weaken the strong man in the Kremlin.

On the other hand, the Russian head of state has above all shown the Western world that he no longer intends to open to diplomacy to have preconditions imposed on him. This is undoubtedly what the Atlantic alliance and the leaders of its member states lacked. Russia has provoked to impose a balance of power. It showed that it was ready to intervene to demonstrate its determination to carry out military operations while remaining open to dialogue. However, the latter had to take place under certain conditions. Russia is standing up to the Western world in a way for which it has joined actions to words. It did not attack Ukraine by surprise. Everyone was warned and was considering the scenario of a military operation. What are the reactions to these denounced attacks? The number one option is economic sanctions. This brings us into the debate on culture shock. Russians and other Westerners do not perceive the balance of power in the same way. When Vladimir Putin shows himself ready to fight on the ground, the adversaries see the duel differently. Armed confrontation should only be the option of last resort, especially since the master of the Kremlin seems to face unexpected difficulties from the very first hours of combat.

The President of the Russian Federation may have made mistakes, according to Hubert Védrine, but our feeling is that he has won his bet by creating disorder. By "winning", we must understand that he has challenged the Western world and expects to obtain satisfaction, despite the criticism, because he has put in check any form of adverse reaction likely to make him abandon his desire to conquer. However, he has never closed the door to dialogue. He played the game. The West wanted to intimidate him and set conditions for negotiation. He responded by announcing that he would intervene. He was very consistent in the way he communicated. He had confirmation that the Atlantic alliance feared the scenario of an armed confrontation with Russia as well as an unpreparedness for war. However, it is not clear that Vladimir Putin will emerge victorious from Ukraine. He has succeeded in carrying out his threats. Armed confrontation is now a reality, but there is no indication that his plans are working as he wishes.

Some people refer to Vladimir Putin's irrationality, recalling that he considers the fall of the USSR to be the greatest geopolitical catastrophe of the 20th century. Is this episode, which marked the end of the Cold War, so painful as to make him a man inhabited by a sick obsession that makes him lose control of his sense of reality? Nothing is less certain. On closer inspection, this umpteenth crisis opposing Russia and Ukraine is nothing new. On the other hand, since he took office in 2000, tensions between Moscow and Kiev have been on the rise. What the Western world sees as the annexation of Crimea, a view of the problem perceived differently by Russia, could suggest that the Kremlin would not stop at this peninsula. At the time of the facts, let's remember these icy relations with Barack Obama then President of the United States and whose number two was none other than Joe Biden. Let's also remember the support given by Hillary Clinton in person to the demonstrators on Maidan Square in Kiev. There were the many controversies that marked the 2016 presidential election in the United States. Moreover, this affair retains many shadowy areas, both on the Russian and American sides. There were undoubtedly campaigns of Russian cyberattacks against Hillary Clinton, but on the Democratic side, there was probably a certain ease in sticking all possible evils to Russia, such as possibly suspecting Donald Trump of being in the pay of Russia. The latter has always been an ardent defender of his country's interests. As for his relations with Russia, it is difficult to accuse him of any complacency with Moscow.

In sum, the current Ukrainian crisis comes during Democratic governance in the United States, a few weeks after the end of Angela Merkel's long reign in Germany, a year after the Brexit, and a few weeks before a presidential election in France in which President Macron will be playing for re-election. Once again, all of this also comes after the catastrophic departure of the coalition forces from Afghanistan summoned by the Taliban to leave Kabul as soon as possible. Vladimir Putin has carefully studied the institutional, military, and other weaknesses of the Western world. At the risk of being wrong, we tend to think that Vladimir Putin is rational. He is probably more willing to take risks than his opponents, and that is how he intimidates them. Can we believe that simple economic sanctions will succeed in dissuading him from stopping his armies in Ukraine? No, no and no! Vladimir Putin proposes a military provocation and is opposed by economic sanctions? If his intervention in Ukraine is to be criticized and condemned, there should be no mistake: the Western world has its share of responsibility in the matter. On February 24, an article published in the French newspaper Le Figaro made a critical but well-founded presentation of Western weakness, stating that Vladimir Putin *"is counting on the passivity of Europe, soft and divided, reticent by principle or habit."* [31] Russia is acting while the Western camp is only reacting. The military operations carried out in Ukraine are shocking in the eyes of the Atlantic alliance, but they came at a time

---

[31] Isabelle Lasserre, *"Guerre en Ukraine: pourquoi Poutine n'a plus peur de personne"*, www.lefigaro.fr, February 24, 2022 Translation done by the author from French quote.

when Vladimir Putin felt in a position of strength. He did not attack at any time. Why would he not advance to Kiev since no one is opposed to him except the Ukrainian armed forces? The message is violent: Russia shows that it fears no one and that it is ruthlessly challenging Western authority.

Everything that is happening in Ukraine is the result of careful consideration. The Kremlin did not order such an offensive by chance. It is said that President Putin is acting dangerously, that he is driven by megalomaniac ambitions and obsessive disorder. In the meantime, he does not procrastinate. He attacks and presents the Atlantic alliance with a fait accompli. The latter was slow to react. However, the Russian head of state has carefully prepared the ground for a long time. He advanced his pawns while the opposing camp sought a diplomatic solution, while continuing to threaten the Kremlin with sanctions. This is not the way to gain Russia's respect and consideration. Moscow was willing to listen as long as it was not given the impression that it was indicating a form of Western superiority. The Western world has not kept in mind the timeline of events in 2014 with the Crimea crisis that erupted at the end of February, then the start of the Donbass war a few weeks later... and the signing of a giant hydrocarbon agreement between Russia and China in May. This means that Moscow and Beijing had already been negotiating the terms of this four hundred-billion-dollar energy deal for some time. Russia had just sealed the way around the economic sanctions imposed by the West and shifted its commercial center of gravity to the East. Above all, this means that Moscow had prepared the political and economic ground with Beijing before getting involved in the Crimea and Donbass crises.

The parallel is striking in view of the events of February 2022. China and Russia jointly declared their disapproval of NATO and Ankus territorial expansion in the Indo-Pacific region. Three weeks later, Moscow went on the offensive as Beijing looked on incredulously. The difference is that the intensity of the crisis this time is greater than in 2014. This resemblance leads us to believe that everything has been carefully prepared and that the Russian attitude towards the Atlantic alliance is to indicate to it that the era of its total domination over major international issues is now over. Not only does Vladimir Putin no longer fear anyone, but he feels so strong that he is the master of the game in the Ukrainian crisis, or at least he thinks so. His opponents are slow to retaliate, and he continues to advance to Kiev without blinking. This time, it is he who is proposing the opportunity for negotiation, but he is imposing the rules of the game. From our point of view, everything seems to indicate that he remains a rational, tactical, and strategic state leader. On the other hand, this does not guarantee that he will get what he wants. Despite this, he is facing unexpected opposition in Ukraine. If the Russian armed forces succeed in destroying targeted infrastructure, they will not easily take Kiev, where the local army can count on the reinforcement of many volunteers who are giving the enemy a hard time.

On February 26 and 27, tensions between Russia and NATO took on a new tragic dimension when the Kremlin summarily declared that it had put its nuclear deterrent forces on alert. Vladimir Putin has thus brandished the nuclear threat... while the Russian army is facing difficulties in Ukraine. The Ukrainian armed opposition is indeed tending to organize itself and is inflicting losses on the Russian side. In the Western camp, the comments are rife: if Russia has nuclear force, the United States, the United Kingdom, and France also have it. Once again, the opposing camps are testing and evaluating each other. In this game, it is the master of the Kremlin who always outbids them. After all, hadn't he proposed to Kiev a negotiation on the condition that the Ukrainian army lay down its arms? The situation is changing by the hour. The nuclear threat comes at a time when the Russian army has just conquered the Chernobyl region, as a symbol. Russia is determined to go beyond the scenario anticipated by the West, i.e., an invasion of the separatist regions. Kiev is in Moscow's sights. Vladimir Putin has embarked on a communication operation that has led to fears of the worst and made some detractors say that he has gone mad or that he is paranoid.

As for the Western alliance, it has struck hard by strengthening its arsenal of sanctions. European airspace is now off limits to Russian airlines. Russia has been banned from the SWIFT platform, an international interbank network. This latest sanction should deal a severe blow to the Russian economy. Moreover, on February 28, at the opening of the European financial markets, the national currency lost 30% of its value against the dollar. Finally, isn't the main threat to Russia coming from inside? The question arises even more because there is indeed a protest movement in Russia.

At the United Nations, during a meeting on climate, a Russian delegate apologized on behalf of all Russians and expressed admiration for the Ukrainian delegation attending the meeting. This is a powerful gesture from a Russian official. Above all, it shows that the Kremlin's decisions are not validated by everyone in Russia. This event, which occurred on February 27, may have influenced the holding of bipartisan negotiations in Belarus, starting February 28, which include Ukraine and Russia. While the hypothetical use of nuclear force is not a threat to be taken lightly, it would appear that Russian plans are not unfolding as Vladimir Putin had hoped. Yet these signs indicate that Russia is having doubts and may have overestimated its ability to conquer Ukraine should not obscure another reality: no foreign power has ever allowed itself to challenge Western dominance with such a degree of provocation. Some will see the Western alliance as a collective force that has proven effective against Russian threats. Others will see the Russian attitude as a sign of a change in international relations: Western domination can be challenged. Russia has acted. Finally, on China's side, one is closely observing the evolution of the situation in Eastern Europe.

From our point of view, we have not been convinced by the defense capabilities of the Atlantic alliance, which has certainly given its support to President Zelensky. It does not intend to engage in an armed struggle against Russian forces on Ukrainian territory. This is undoubtedly a well-considered strategy, but the question remains: would NATO be afraid to engage in an armed struggle against Russia? Would it be prepared for it? Fortunately, the scenario of a Russia-NATO war seems to be receding despite the nuclear threat. On the other hand, the Russian attitude towards Ukraine will remain a scar, that is to say a visible trace, for the whole of the Western world, which had not been put to such a severe test for a long time.

Once again, there are several possible readings. The first is to say that the Ukrainian crisis has strengthened ties within the EU and NATO. This is undoubtedly the case, as the predominant impression is of a spirit of cohesion. The second is more critical. It concerns the attitude of President Biden, who has failed in his diplomatic endeavors, and the time taken by the Western alliance to react to Russian intimidation and actions. Moreover, when President

Zelensky, who refused the Western proposal for exfiltration and safety, asked that the EU integrates his country as soon as possible among its member states, we are entitled to wonder whether Brussels will accept so easily to make a country that shares so many borders with Russia join. In short, is it in Brussels' interest to have Ukraine in its ranks? The question arises all the more because Ukraine does indeed benefit from logistical support from the West, but would the latter go so far as to send Russia back on the ropes by making the affront of integrating Ukraine as the twenty-eighth member state and "ensuring" increasingly tense relations with Moscow? But the accession process would still have to be set in motion. The statement of the President of the European Commission Ursula von der Leyen on Euronews about Ukraine, in which she confesses that it is close to the EU and that it will become a full member in the future [32], should be considered with caution. She was only expressing an opinion, a personal one, while making it clear that this is a long-term vision. Ukraine's accession to the EU remains conditional on legal texts that define the conditions of entry for any new member. President Zelensky immediately declared that he was in favor of his country joining "without delay". Obviously, his wish will not be granted soon.

Vladimir Putin has undoubtedly made several mistakes concerning his Ukrainian ambitions and the discontent of Russians (military and civilians, for the moment still a minority it seems) who do not approve of this military operation. Does all this make him an irrational man? Our answer is no. He attacked in the separatist regions and then on a larger scale because it was his intention to disturb the Western world, to do battle with it and probably

---

[32] Jérôme Cristiani, *"Von der Leyen veut l'Ukraine dans l'UE (« Ils sont des nôtres»)*, *Zelensky répond : oui, tout de suite ! "*, www.latribune.fr, February 28, 2022

to test its power. In some respects, whatever the outcome of the Ukrainian crisis, he will have succeeded in part. He will probably not get what he wanted in Ukraine, but he has disturbed the peace of the Western world. In any case, he will have shown China that it can in turn be vindictive towards the West and the Aukus alliance, especially in the Indo-Pacific area. Would it not be in the common interest of Moscow and Beijing to destabilize the political and economic leadership of the Western world?

Homeric anger of President Biden... and communication blunders?
March 2022

March 26-27, 2022, a little over a month after the fighting in Ukraine began, President Joe Biden's patience reached its limit. During several statements made to the media, he got carried away to the point of calling his Russian alter ego a "dictator" or a "butcher", words that are very rarely used in international politics. Worse, he even went so far as to confide that a change in the head of Russia's governance had to be thought of... suggesting that an overthrow of Vladimir Putin could be imagined. This comment was probably inappropriate, since the White House communicated in turn to keep up appearances and indicate that Joe Biden's thinking was not to imagine a plan to remove the Russian President from power.

As a result, Joe Biden went too far and did not control his communication. However, there is substance and form. On the form, he was clumsy. For the White House to react in such a way by making clarifications, it is certain that the intervention of its author was not the most opportune in terms of its content. The French head of state declared shortly afterwards that he would not have communicated in the same way, thus tactfully implying that he did not agree with the words of his American colleague. On the other hand, on the substance, the President of the United States expressed an anger that he no longer conceals and above all showed a determination to fight with Vladimir Putin. The latter continues to threaten peace in the world? The West, with the United States in the lead, will take it upon itself to show him that he is not the strongest and even less the master of the game! For Joe Biden, these communications tend to show that he is the man driven by an unfailing determination to fight the arrogance of the Kremlin.

The head of the American executive branch has taken his communication up a notch. This is his way of showing the world that he will not be influenced by Vladimir Putin. It is also an opportunity to show his critics in the United States that he is not the soft man so often described. He cannot let Russia continue its war efforts in Ukraine with impunity. Moreover, it is now time for Washington to show its intransigence towards Moscow.

The differences between the two capitals are old. Beyond these unfriendly and reciprocal feelings that recall the scent of the Cold War of yesteryear, the United States intends to put Russia to the sword, where the latter has been widely criticized in recent years for its campaigns of subversion, espionage, provocation, and other means deployed to wage this hybrid war with the Western world. The Atlantic alliance seems determined to take a firm stand against the actions of the Kremlin and the Gerasimov Doctrine, named after the Chief of Staff of the Russian Armed Forces, who set up this hybrid war. Joe Biden has not forgotten the icy climate that animated the meetings between Barack Obama and Vladimir Putin. Nor has he forgotten the 2016 electoral campaign for which a number of compromising emails concerning the Democratic Party and Hillary Clinton, then the candidate announced as the favorite of the election against the inexperienced Donald Trump, were leaked. We know what happened next. American resentments against Russia are numerous and Washington has obviously decided to blow the whistle on the end game. The Western world does not respond to Russia on the ground of military confrontation but has opted for a strategy that aims to weaken it economically to better destabilize it.

By venturing into Ukraine, Vladimir Putin has gone too far. No doubt he considered it his duty to attack since no one resisted him in 2014 with the Crimea affair and then the war in Donbass. Similarly, when he intervened to support Syrian leader Bashar al-Assad, despite Western discontent, no one resisted him enough to make him think twice and turn back. If left to his own devices, he will continue to advance and provoke. He is said to have had inordinate ambitions, driven by an unyielding desire to restore the empire of the Tsars. More prosaically, he has made sure to tell the world that Russia must be treated as an equal with the Western camp at any negotiating table, that it is one of the major political powers on the planet. As for Ukraine, it has been in his sights since he has been piloting Russia. In his eyes, Kiev is too close to the West and the United States in particular. This thought is unbearable for him. Similarly, Ukraine should not join the European Union... and even less NATO.

The Atlantic alliance still refuses to engage in an armed conflict with Russia. After four weeks of fighting in Ukraine, the Russian army is encountering difficulties that it had clearly not foreseen. Vladimir Putin finds himself in a deadlock: he cannot leave the country and risk losing the war. He has no choice but to continue what he has started. Although negotiations with Ukraine are taking place in Turkey, it is clear that neither side will agree to the demands of the other. President Zelensky is determined to drive the Russian enemy out of the country. Although he has not obtained what he is asking for, namely a human military presence of NATO in Ukraine, he can count on important logistical and financial support. This allows the national army and the many fighters who have come to lend a hand to the latter to resist and counter the Russian offensives.

In the Ukrainian issue, Vladimir Putin has always shown the image of a man who wants to play the role of the master of the game. He probably did not foresee that his military operation would encounter so many difficulties. The initial idea was for a blitzkrieg that would last no more than two weeks. The objective was missed. These setbacks on the ground explain in part the Kremlin's communication on the nuclear threat. The latter is indeed the ultimate weapon, the one that can seal the fate of Ukraine and the difficult relations that Russia has with the Western world. The Atlantic alliance does not intend to give in to pressure. It has understood that Vladimir Putin is facing unforeseen difficulties. Thus, the harsh and unusual words used by Joe Biden sound like a message addressed to the Russian leader: he has unleashed the unthinkable, which everyone in the West feared; he will now have to assume the consequences.

The duel between the Western alliance and Russia promises to be bitter. If the White House has intervened to clarify the remarks made by Joe Biden, make no mistake about it. There is probably some truth in what was said. For him, the world would gain if a change of political governance and regime were to occur in Russia. In terms of protocol communication, this is a mistake. He should not have expressed himself in this way. On the other hand, in view of the circumstances of the Ukrainian crisis and the Western feelings towards President Putin, no one will hold it against him. Moreover, we wonder: if the White House reacted quickly to put an end to the controversy, were President Biden's remarks not intentional? After all, such a statement is a direct message to the Kremlin. It is not only a message to Russia that the Atlantic alliance will continue its efforts to thwart Russian intentions; if Vladimir Putin does not emerge victorious from this confrontation, it will be difficult for him to remain in power. Joe Biden's remarks were certainly intentional, if awkward. Above all, they show that he will do his best to destabilize his Russian counterpart. The message has been sent.

Not surprisingly, the Kremlin took exception to the presidential comments, calling them "alarming. In the wake of this, President Biden reaffirmed that he did not take back anything he had said, which forced the White House to communicate urgently. He said that he was expressing personal indignation rather than any opinion suggesting the idea of an overthrow of power in Russia. He defended himself by indicating that he was in favor of Vladimir Putin's departure from power. This did not fail to cause a reaction both in the West and in Russia.

By attacking the Russian chief executive in this way, even though he is expressing a personal opinion, he is further straining an already anxiety-provoking atmosphere, as Moscow interprets these remarks as an expression of a thinly veiled intention to incite political change in Russia. At the same time, it only confirms the reality of diplomatic relations between Russia and the United States. In other words, the Ukrainian crisis is the perfect opportunity for Joe Biden to destabilize Vladimir Putin and put him in trouble. However, he did not rule out the idea of a meeting with his Russian counterpart, while specifying that it would depend on what the latter would have to offer. This is a way of putting the pressure back on the Russian side. Clearly, he will accept a meeting only if he is in a position of strength.

Through this communication from Joe Biden, we understand that the big maneuvers are underway while the negotiations between Ukraine and Russia continue in Turkey. According to the media, both sides seem inclined to make concessions to make the discussions evolve favorably. Joe Biden's high-profile interventions are not innocent.

They are not intended to add fuel to the fire to make these negotiations fail, but they aim to embarrass Russia. The latter is facing military difficulties on the ground. The Ukrainian armed opposition is resistant. Russians and Ukrainians undoubtedly share an interest: to ensure that the armed struggle does not drag on. Therefore, it is logical that both sides seek to agree on negotiated terms to calm the hostilities. Joe Biden's communications come in this sensitive context: if Russia is ready to make concessions to Ukraine, Kiev will have to make the most of them.

In conclusion, appearances can sometimes be deceiving. It is possible that President Biden has made gross miscommunications by directly attacking Vladimir Putin in this way. In such a case, the fears expressed by some Western leaders that the peace negotiations would be compromised are justified. However, another reading is possible. The choice of words is perhaps calculated. While the White House quickly intervened to clear up any misunderstanding and controversy, we cannot rule out the possibility that Joe Biden did not intentionally communicate in this way in order to thwart Russia's negotiating strategy with Ukraine and to indicate to the latter that it must be intransigent in the conditions of the current negotiations. As for Joe Biden's personal opinion, it is probably sincere. He would not oppose Vladimir Putin's departure, but he cannot provoke him by suggesting it as he did: in international law, this is called interference. In this case, it would be an external intervention that would be carried out without the consent of Russia and that would go against the sovereignty of the State. This is why we believe that the real message sent by Joe Biden is not intended to incite the overthrow of Vladimir Putin. Rather, we imagine that it is part of what we might call the "symmetry of the unthinkable". When President Putin unleashed the nuclear threat, the shock wave was great because he had dared to brandish the possibility of a war that would then take on another dimension. Perhaps in the face of such a threat, Joe Biden simply wanted to retaliate with another threat that was just as "unimaginable": no one had ever dared to express one's desire to see Vladimir Putin leave the Kremlin. In short, the communication blows of the President of the United States surprised everyone, starting with Moscow. Perhaps this was the effect sought by its author. We give him the benefit of the doubt.

War in Eastern Europe and soaring oil prices
April 2022

March 7 of 2022 will remain a historic date. Ten days after the outbreak of hostilities in Ukraine by the Russian army, crude oil trading prices briefly approached $140 per barrel for Brent. Such a level had not been reached for almost fifteen years. At the time, it was an all-time high. For several years, crude oil prices have been rather low. The crisis in the Ukraine and the outbreak of war caused a surge in prices. This crisis situation quickly generated fears in the financial markets. Apart from the problems of production failure or black gold supply, what about a possible tightening of economic sanctions against Russia? The question is not insignificant, especially since Russia is one of the three largest producers in the world and exports almost half of its production, which in 2021 was more than eleven million five hundred thousand barrels per day. Russia is therefore a major player in the global oil market. The outbreak of hostilities in Ukraine was therefore followed by adverse effects for consumers. The risk of an oil shortage quickly emerged to worry and panic the international markets. Thus, demand suddenly increased and induced a sharp rise in exchange prices.

For crude oil importers, this price spike is obviously not good news. In many jurisdictions, the price of gasoline has exploded. In France, it is now two euros, whereas such a price level seemed unthinkable until recently. Gasoline has become a luxury consumer good that many French people can no longer afford. This topic is being debated by the candidates for the presidential election to be held in April 2022. Many public and private actors contest the price increase; others, on the contrary, are delighted. For producers, both public and private, selling at such a high price is a boon. Some hope that the economic sanctions imposed on Russia will soon affect hydrocarbon exports. If Moscow were to stop exporting, others would jump at the chance to increase their production and take market share. With such high exchange prices, it goes without saying that the expected economic benefits are a jackpot.

Two months after the beginning of the war in Ukraine, the Atlantic alliance seems more united than ever against Russia. All its members agree to intensify their arsenal of sanctions against Moscow. The objective is clear: to exert maximum pressure on the Russian economy. Thus, the strategy is to avoid any form of military intervention and to focus on weakening the Russian economy, which would put Vladimir Putin in difficulty. However, there is dissension in Europe about the sanctions that could be imposed on Russian hydrocarbons. Within the European Union (EU), there is a debate. The general trend is that economic sanctions against Moscow should be intensified. When it comes to oil and gas, there are two main categories: those who want to attack Russian hydrocarbon imports and those who prefer not to touch them.

The European energy reality is simple when it comes to oil and gas consumption. Part of the supply comes from Russia. The dependence of EU member states differs according to their geographical location. The countries of Central and Eastern Europe are mainly supplied with Russian hydrocarbons. However, the latter are firmly opposed to Russia and are in favor of sanctions against Russian hydrocarbon imports. This is not the case for everyone. Germany does not share this view but may change its mind due to the discovery of horrors committed against the civilian population in the Kiev region. These abuses are attributed to Russian troops. Several investigations have been launched to try to understand what happened and especially who committed these atrocities.

Western suspicions are that the massacres were orchestrated by the Russian army (the decision of an officer on the ground or an order from the highest Russian authorities, the question arises). Faced with the discovery of such desolate scenes, Germany seems ready to reconsider its position on Russian hydrocarbon imports.

On April 7, 2022, the EU announced a new package of sanctions. One of them was an embargo on Russian coal imports starting in August 2022. This was the first time Brussels had directly attacked energy supplies. It may have been a harbinger of the possibility of further sanctions on Russian oil and gas. The European Parliament was in favor of this. Until now, the oil and gas industry has only been penalized upstream, i.e., not in terms of deliveries. The Bucha massacres could change this.

On April 8, a missile strike hit the railway station in the Donbass town of Kramatorsk, while many civilians were crowded on the platforms hoping to catch a train out of the region. The missile killed several dozen people and injured about one hundred. This event once again caused outrage. The missile strike was attributed to Russia, which a few days earlier had opted for a change in military strategy by focusing its war efforts on the Eastern part of Ukraine. If the investigation confirms the Russian origin of the strike, such an event could trigger the implementation of a new arsenal of sanctions targeting Moscow. Russian oil and gas shipments could be targeted.

Oil at the heart of many international crises and issues
If Russian hydrocarbons are attracting so much attention from the Atlantic alliance, the reason is simple: the Russian economic model is partly based on the sale of these raw materials. Russia is one of the world's hydrocarbon giants. For the Western camp, as soon as the response

strategy was aimed at attacking the Russian economy, the international markets immediately began to worry about the consequences of sanctions on Russian oil and the disruption that could be caused to world supply. Prices immediately soared. Fears about supplies, possible future economic sanctions and the duration of the Ukrainian conflict also influenced a speculative effect bordering on frenzy. Brent crude oil briefly traded around $140 per barrel, whereas since 2016 it had twice traded below $30. It is certain that the impact on the financial markets would not have been the same if it had been a much smaller producer. In this case, Russia is one of the world's three largest producers of crude oil. The fact that it was attacking a neighboring country supported by the Western world soon sent the financial sector into a panic.

The crisis in Ukraine reminds us that despite the international community's sustained efforts to engage in an energy transition aimed at reducing its dependence on fossil resources, black gold remains the most influential natural resource in international relations. This had been true for the past century. Oil has always been directly or indirectly associated with the major crises of the 20th century. We can cite the two World Wars in which it played a central role: anyone who could no longer satisfy their oil needs would be condemned to defeat. This is what earned the former French statesman Georges Clémenceau a famous reflection for which he considered that a drop of oil was worth a drop of blood. He was referring to the crucial importance of oil during the First World War. This was confirmed in the Second World War. Nazi Germany was engaged in Russia in order to gain access to Azerbaijan's oil reserves in the Caspian Sea. It never succeeded. The shortage of oil supplies for the German army helped to change the course of the war. What about the importance of oil during the Cold War and the rise of the OPEC cartel? The oil shocks of 1973 and 1979 occurred because the producers of black gold understood its importance for the world economy. It was such that the slightest disturbance in the financial markets sent the world into a tizzy. For a producer, it was enough to announce its desire to disrupt supply to make itself heard. This is what OPEC did in the 1970s. Prices soared while the cartel voluntarily reduced its supply. In the 1980s, the opposite was true. An alliance sealed with the Western camp agreed to open the floodgates of production in order to flood the world with oil... and to drown the dying Soviet economy, whose model was based in part on sales of black gold. We tend to forget this, but oil had a major impact on the outcome of the Cold War. It precipitated it.

What was the first post-Cold War international crisis? The invasion of Kuwait by Iraq. This led to the first Gulf War. Oil was once again a central issue in this crisis. The Iraqi army set fire to nearly seven hundred oil wells in Kuwait. As a reminder, Saddam Hussein felt he had been wronged by his Western allies at the end of the long conflict between his country and Iran. He wanted to "pay back" by invading neighboring Kuwait and by taking advantage of its abundant oil reserves. The Western world, led by the United States, did not see it that way. A coalition intervened and engaged in an armed struggle against Iraqi troops who were unable to compete with the enemy. This Gulf War marked a new phase in international relations with the end of the Cold War. A new world order took shape with the affirmation of American ultra-domination over the world.

In the 1990s, as China's need for oil increased, it was forced to look abroad to meet its domestic demand. In the 2000s, China's economic rise was linked to its oil consumption. For the Bush Administration, it was obvious that China could no longer access oil so easily. In Beijing, it became essential to diversify strategic partnerships in order to ensure the imports necessary for the country's economic functioning. Strategic partnerships multiplied in Africa, South America, and other regions. In the eyes of the United States, the best way to hinder China's economic rise was to disrupt its black gold supplies. This has never stopped China from meeting its domestic needs. Worse, its rise to power has manifested itself through the strategic alliance concluded with Iran in 2021, a country hated by the United States, which will allow China to buy Iranian oil for twenty-five years. The Chinese example, among many others, is a perfect illustration of the geopolitical stakes that revolve around oil.

National interests and geopolitical issues

In two years, the oil sector has gone through all kinds of states. In April 2020, the US benchmark, WTI, experienced a collapse in barrel trading prices and reached a negative value. Such a scenario stunned the financial world. A -$37 trading price could not be expected. This meant that an inventory holder was forced to pay a buyer to offload his barrels. Although the situation was short-lived, it was significant. The world market had just experienced an unprecedented disruption caused by the combination of two factors: firstly, the Covid-19 health crisis, which had had a strong impact on world oil demand, while for a time, supply had not adapted to real needs. The world economy was slowed down by the spread of the pandemic, but the oil sector continued to produce abundantly. Many stocks could no longer be sold. Worse still, the world had another concern: what about the threat of storage capacity saturation? Indeed, the question was raised for some time. In a rush, some stockholders wanted to get rid of barrels that could not be sold as quickly as possible. This had a strong downward impact on oil prices. Secondly, in March 2020, a disagreement arose between Saudi Arabia and

Russia, two of the world's three largest oil producers, regarding the production policy of black gold within the OPEC + alliance in order to halt the inexorable fall in exchange prices. The aim of Riyadh was to convince Moscow to commit to a policy of lowering production in order to reduce global supply. Russia refused. The Wahhabi kingdom then embarked on an aggressive price policy that resulted in a sharp drop in trading prices.

Covid and disagreement on production policy within OPEC soon disrupted a market already facing recurring difficulties, particularly since the introduction of shale oil by the United States on the international markets. The exploitation of these non-conventional oils has the particularity of requiring less investment to exploit the raw material while the return on investment is much faster than for a so-called conventional deposit. Thus, the United States, which had abundant reserves of shale oil, took advantage of this to increase its production capacity. They were thus able to start exporting part of their production, whereas the country used to devote its production to domestic consumption. Also, given the economic model for exploiting these unconventional oils, American producers could sell their production at a much lower price than conventional oils... while making significant profits. During the Trump presidency, the White House's objective was to impact the selling price of black gold downwards in order to guarantee low prices for certain by-products such as gasoline to the American consumer. This strategy was also intended to weaken the national economic model of the main competitors: Saudi Arabia and Russia.

Since 2016, black gold trading prices were unfavorable to producers. For some, the survival of their business was at stake. The eruption of the Covid-19 brought unexpected consequences, or at least they were expected to some extent. The large-scale downturn in activity led to a sharp drop in global oil demand. Supply did not immediately adjust to the market reality and resulted in a glut of oil on the world market. For this sector of activity, the convalescence was long. Gradually, prices recovered and stabilized around $60 to $70. The outbreak of the war in Ukraine had an immediate impact on prices. It was immediately feared that a prolonged crisis could have unfortunate consequences on available supply and supply channels. Panic took hold of the financial markets and trading prices soared. They quickly exceeded $100 and approached $140 for a barrel of Brent.

In such a situation, there are happy players and less happy ones. For the producers, selling oil at such a high price was unhoped-for. Thus, they had to take advantage of it! For the buyers, it was going to considerably inflate the energy bill. When the possibility of sanctioning Russian hydrocarbons began to circulate in Washington and Brussels, some saw the opportunity to gain market shares "abandoned" by Russia. The hunt for profits was on! The specter of possible extended sanctions against Russian hydrocarbon exports whetted the appetite of producers who imagined they could take advantage of an unprecedented context with trading prices that had not been reached for a decade.

For Russia, the imposition of new economic sanctions on oil and gas exports would have dramatic consequences. On March 8, 2022, President Biden announced an embargo on Russian oil imports. In Europe, the attitude of Russia in Ukraine exasperates some leaders who call for the most severe sanctions on Russian hydrocarbons. This concerns in particular countries that depend heavily on Russian supplies. As we have already seen, this thinking is not unanimous within the EU.

Moreover, after several weeks of fighting, it seems likely that the armed opposition will continue. In the meantime, the panic effect observed on the financial markets has faded. The armed conflict in Eastern Europe must now be dealt with. This means that solutions are being thought of to ensure the necessary production on a global scale in case the war is prolonged. This also includes other issues such as the transportation and distribution of oil. As a result, trading prices have fallen. By mid-April 2022, since the beginning of the month, they remained high but stabilized around $100 to $110 per barrel for both Brent and WTI. They were less volatile than in March when there was much more uncertainty. The fact that Russia did not manage to achieve the war objectives it had set itself undoubtedly helped to lower the "alert level", i.e., to calm down the speculators who had rushed to buy crude oil a fortnight after the start of hostilities in Ukraine. A wave of panic accompanied the financial markets when the first echoes of potential sanctions on Russian exports began to circulate in Europe. This is all the more understandable given that Russia is the EU's largest supplier of oil, accounting for 27%, while any other European partner accounts for less than 10% of oil imports. Thus, a question nagged at speculators: how would the EU compensate for its oil needs in the event of sanctions against Russia? The specter of a supply deficit or even a shortage seized the financial markets, especially as Europe was also experiencing supply problems for many consumer goods... which resulted in a sharp increase in prices for the end consumer.

The EU is urging its member states to plan for diversification of their energy suppliers, with natural gas at the forefront, since some of them depend almost exclusively on Russian gas imports for this market. In international relations, any dependence is associated with a danger. In this case, for the EU, the danger was to be too dependent on

Russian hydrocarbon imports and to find itself unable to compensate for what would no longer be purchased from Russia. The best way to show Russia that sanctions on oil and gas imports would not be detrimental to the EU is to ensure that these energy needs can be met with other suppliers. This has contributed to the panic in the financial markets. Moreover, it should be remembered that the twenty-seven members of this union of states do not share a unanimous opinion on the level of sanctions that should be imposed on Russian fossil fuel exports. However, should the EU announce sanctions on Russian oil and gas supplies, Moscow has already warned that Russia will turn to China and other jurisdictions. One imagines, however, that Brussels would not risk sanctioning Russia in this way without first ensuring that each of its members is certain to meet its oil and gas needs. In other words, it is not such a sanction that would inflame the financial markets too much. The effects would be felt in the very short term. On the other hand, while the war continues to rage, another factor may influence oil trading prices. For the time being, it could drive prices down.

War in Ukraine and new influence of Covid

The Ukrainian conflict seems set to last. All the ingredients are there for this crisis to last. Russia thought it could crush its neighbor by carrying out a rapid intervention that would be punctuated by success. This has not happened. As for Ukraine, it is fighting bitterly against the Russian armed forces to the point that the Kremlin has opted for another strategy: to concentrate its war effort in the Eastern part of the country. In the meantime, the Western world has begun to talk about war crimes committed by Russia. In mid-April, the accusations took on a new dimension: President Joe Biden is now denouncing a genocide perpetrated by Moscow. This communication has been accompanied by a rise in the price of black gold due to supply-side fears. Indeed, the use of the word *genocide* suggests that new economic sanctions could be imposed on Russia and that these would impact global supply.

Every day, new dramatic discoveries are made in Ukraine and are systematically attributed to Russia. After the images showing numerous Ukrainian civilian victims in the streets of cities deserted by Russian troops, which is why the Western world points to them as the perpetrators of these horrors, Russia is now suspected of having used chemical weapons in Mariupol. All this contributes to prolonging the war in Ukraine. The accusations are extremely serious, and it is hard to imagine that Kiev and Moscow will be able to find common ground to calm the hostilities. The armed struggle will continue.

President Putin has no choice but to continue the war. It is impossible for him to give up his arms without risking losing his power in Russia. As for his Ukrainian counterpart, he would never accept a halt to the fighting under conditions that would penalize his country. He is fiercely determined to fight his adversary and he hopes to achieve victory. His Western partners continue to deliver arms and military equipment. They continue to release funds to help the Ukrainian war effort. The strategy remains unchanged: no military intervention for NATO but the implementation of a strategy to weaken the Russian economy through a costly war for the latter and the imposition of heavy economic sanctions.

The war in Ukraine is therefore set to last. It has its share of uncertainties. No one can be sure of winning it. Uncertainty is obviously one of the great fears of the financial markets. This concern is reflected in higher oil prices. In effect, it means that buyers will be looking to buy inventory while supply does not match actual demand or that markets are anticipating a possible future decline in overall supply and / or significant demand. In other words, trading prices rise when supply is scarce relative to demand. What is scarce is expensive.

However, despite all the uncertainties generated by the war, another factor is influencing the price of black gold downwards: Covid. This form of coronavirus has definitely not disappeared from circulation. It continues to evolve and despite vaccination campaigns promoted around the world, it continues to be rampant. One country is in the process of imposing new periods of confinement of the population: China. Such a decision has been adopted in Shanghai in particular, where part of the population has been called upon to stay at home due to numerous cases of contamination. For several weeks, the Chinese authorities have been worried about the high number of new cases of Covid revealed every day. At the time of writing, the health situation in China is worrying enough for us to imagine that the spread of Covid is not limited to the Shanghai area.

If several tens or even hundreds of millions of people had to be confined, this would lead to a slowdown in national economic activity. This has already happened in 2020. China reduced its demand for oil at that time. Considering that it is the world's largest importer of black gold, a sharp slowdown in its demand was quickly reflected in the financial markets. This trend was accentuated when the Western world was forced to confine its populations and consequently experience a slowdown in economic activity. The immediate consequence was a drop in demand for oil. This precipitated a sharp drop in the trading price of black gold. In a few weeks, the world demand collapsed while the supply remained consequent and inadequate to the real demand.

A prolonged Covid crisis in China could have disastrous consequences for Russia. Indeed, if Chinese oil demand were to fall significantly, the trading prices of black gold would tend to fall. The latter are high because supply is lower than demand. If the Covid crisis were to impact global demand again and lead to a rebalancing of the supply-demand ratio, prices would certainly fall.

If any price is based on this supply-demand relationship, it sometimes deviates from this economic theory when exogenous factors are likely to influence a market disruption. By risk, we mean an announcement effect, a piece of information, a rumor or the formation of a trend resulting in a panic effect that can panic a market at any time. This is particularly true for oil. Its weight and influence are such in the world economy and in international relations that any element that could cause a feared effect can be amplified in the financial markets. In other words, a fear of supply risk, or other issues of heightened concern can affect trading prices even though the threat is not necessarily real. Any threat can be the subject of beliefs, whether well-founded or unfounded. It can be sustained over time. For example, it is enough for a rumor about the possible intentions of a player to attack strategic infrastructures that could disrupt oil production or transportation to a great extent for prices to skyrocket. However, it is entirely possible that the feared scenario will never happen.

On the other hand, if global oil demand again experiences a 2020-like scenario, an overall decline close to ten million barrels per day compared to 2019, it will not prevent a sharp decline in trading prices, despite the war in Ukraine and all the concerns it may raise. As a result, Covid can reshuffle the deck on global oil issues. It may also become the Kremlin's worst fear as its oil revenues fall and the war effort is a huge cost to the national economy.

Conclusion

As France prepares to elect its new President of the Republic, the electoral campaign has been largely overshadowed by the war in Ukraine, which has dominated media coverage for several weeks. However, the twelve candidates who tried their luck in the first round have campaigned. Among the main themes discussed, the purchasing power of the French is the one for which each candidate has made proposals in order to attract a maximum of voters. Thus, some proposed to cap the purchase price of many basic products. Prices have indeed risen considerably since the beginning of the year due to issues related to the transportation of goods and the considerable increase in the price of oil and its derivatives. In France, the price of a liter of gasoline has reached the symbolic threshold of two euros or even more. For many French people, such a price of access is no longer bearable. The same is true for many consumer goods whose prices have risen sharply in supermarkets. All this is happening in the middle of an election campaign to choose the next head of state for the upcoming five years. The price of gasoline is therefore an electoral issue. For modest households, getting around is much more expensive. Many people find it difficult to use their means of transport to work. What is true for France is also true for many other jurisdictions that import most of their oil needs.

Oil is once again at the heart of the major issues of a crisis that is worrying many people. While no one knows how the crisis will end, black gold is causing a lot of trouble, to the point that within the EU, the debate on sanctions against Russian oil and gas imports continues to fuel dissension between those states that want to have a maximum impact on the Russian economy and those more reluctant to hit the latter on what it provides abundantly in Europe. It is not necessarily the countries that are most dependent on Russian hydrocarbons that are least in favor of punishing Moscow the most severely. On the contrary, they are those that are uncompromising with regard to Russia.

The Ukrainian crisis has had a major impact on the surge in oil prices. The price of a barrel has been trading for several weeks at price levels not seen in a decade. For producers, business is good. For buyers of crude oil and consumers of black gold products, the story is different. The prices of many products have risen sharply to the point of being unaffordable for some. Within the Atlantic alliance, while the United States did not hesitate for long to impose an embargo on Russian oil and gas imports, the same cannot be said of Europe. On the Old Continent, people are more concerned about the repercussions on the international oil markets if Russia were to find itself heavily penalized in its exports. The purchasing power of Europeans is an issue that concerns a majority of EU member states. Considering that most of them import most of their oil needs, the consequences for the consumer's finances are important when a barrel is traded at a high price.

On the side of the Western alliance, the other facet of the Ukrainian crisis concerns the desire to asphyxiate the Russian economy as much as possible in order to weaken the position of Vladimir Putin in his country. To do this, it is necessary to attack the most lucrative sectors of activity for the Russian economic model. Oil is one of the Western targets. At the same time, this generates fears in the financial markets and encourages a speculative trend that pushes up exchange prices.

In the West, with the Ukrainian crisis, we almost forgot that the Covid pandemic is still with us. Every day, people continue to die from complications of the disease. Official statistics show that the number of deaths is much lower than in the period before the vaccination campaigns. However, the number of cases of infection in Europe remains very high. The pandemic is not yet over. The health situation is becoming even more worrying as China is now communicating in a way it was not used to in 2020 and 2021. It informs that the cases of contamination are rising sharply. In several regions, re-confinements of the populations have been carried out.

Everyone remembers that global economic activity was slowed as a result of the pandemic that spread around the world. However, such a significant slowdown in economic activity was accompanied by a sharp decline in global demand for oil. In other words, if global demand for black gold were to fall significantly again, trading prices would follow the same trajectory. In this case, the economic consequences for Russia would be catastrophic. The country did not imagine that it would engage in a long-lasting and costly armed intervention. With the arsenal of economic sanctions already deployed against it, a significant drop in oil trading prices would have unfortunate consequences for the Russian economy. As of April 15, 2022, the war in Ukraine is not about to end. Oil trading prices remain high (near or above $100 per barrel of Brent). They may spike again if the EU were to ban Russian oil and gas imports into its jurisdictions. On the other hand, the Covid health crisis is definitely not over. The new confinements decided in China leave one uncertainty: could these confinements soon be promoted on a larger scale at the risk of once again disrupting the smooth functioning of the global economy? Such a hypothesis would reshuffle

many cards, which could also have an impact on the course
of the war in Ukraine.

The horrors of war: from unresolved quarrels to chaos
April 2022

Is it necessary to broadcast unbearable images to evoke the harsh reality of a war? The conflict between Ukraine and Russia is no exception to the rule of the power of images. Dead bodies are shown strewn on the ground, abandoned, some of them burned. Information is pouring in. It is said that the Russian army is suffering considerable military losses. The human toll is very heavy. The logistical losses are just as heavy. Vladimir Putin was forced to change strategy and to concentrate his military efforts in the East of Ukraine. Scenes of horror animate this country that has become a martyr while Moscow and Kiev continue their discussions in Turkey in order to try to find a common ground that would put an end to the hostilities... or at least to try to calm them down for a while. Russia is therefore facing unexpected difficulties from the Kremlin. Many generals and colonels have paid with their lives for this intervention in Ukraine. Never before have so many Russian officers fallen in battle since the Second World War. The scenario was so unforeseen by President Putin that a statement in the form of a confession was made after more than a month of fierce fighting: bad intelligence would have pushed the Russian leader to take decisions with heavy consequences. If there is one certainty, it is precisely that the Kremlin had bet on a lightning war. It failed. It is whispered in the West that the army has never dared to stand up to the wishes of Vladimir Putin for fear of provoking his anger. Thus, one has killed an unpreparedness for war. Many soldiers sent to Ukraine were clearly not prepared to fight. The equipment also suffered. Between the men fallen and wounded in combat and those disillusioned, some of whom have opted for desertion, the Russian commitment in Ukraine seems compromised.

On the other side, the Ukrainian army did more than resist. It has prevented its adversary from advancing at will. Strengthened by a national impulse devoted to the defense of the country, it opposes more than a resistance. It seems stronger than the adversity. On the Ukrainian side, military losses are also numerous. As in every armed conflict, the civilian population is not spared. At the beginning of April 2022, the town of Bucha saw the Russian troops withdraw. The Kiev region began to be depopulated by the Russian army, which was summoned to the Eastern Front. The media quickly relayed images of horror. There is talk of several hundred people being shot by the Russian troops before their departure. The corpses litter the roads devastated by the fighting. Immediately, Ukraine and its Western supporters denounce war crimes. The Atlantic alliance evoked an intensification of sanctions against Russia. Voices are being raised to demand that Russian officials be brought before an international criminal court.

The horror has no limits. Like the great city of Mariupol, Bucha embodies the image of the martyred city. In the West, a unanimous reaction condemns what is supposedly attributed to the Russian army. In this case, the victims are counted in the hundreds or even thousands. No one knows how many civilians died. When Russia claims that it is only attacking strategic and military targets, this is a lie. How many Ukrainian civilians have died in the bombing and other circumstances? Far too many.

As for the armed forces, how many Ukrainian and Russian soldiers and fighters have given their lives? While it is difficult to put forward a reliable human toll, after a month and a half of fighting, many estimates put the number of dead at several tens of thousands. The number of wounded is probably just as high. The Western media report that many Russian soldiers do not understand this war, that they do not support it, that they cannot get used to the idea of fighting an enemy with whom they were brothers in arms during the Second World War and all the conflicts in which the USSR was involved. In the past, Ukrainians and Russians fought side by side. Today, Ukrainians hate Russians. This war will leave lasting traces. On April 5, it is said in the West that the Russian people disapprove of the war. However, in Russia, a poll seems to indicate that Vladimir Putin's popularity is growing and the majority of the people approve of his decisions regarding Ukraine. [33] Who is telling the truth?

While both countries are now seeking to negotiate a diplomatic agreement, we are convinced that such an outcome will not bury the hatchet for good. The evils are far too deep. The hatred will not dissipate by magic. Moreover, what about a possible diplomatic agreement? Would it be accepted by the Ukrainian people? We can ask ourselves this question because it is not certain that they would accept that a part of the national territory could leave the bosom of Kiev. As for Russia, if the military operation does not turn out as it was initially expected, it will not be able to capitulate as if nothing had happened. If Ukraine seems more than ever in a position of strength to negotiate, Moscow has no intention of giving in without obtaining some satisfaction... unless the system collapses from within. By internal collapse, one should understand a global disassociation expressed against Vladimir Putin and his leading team. This would imply that the army would rise up against the Kremlin's orders, that the national population would express its fed up with the situation in view of the human losses and the economic damage caused, or that the economic elites would rise up against the executive power.

---

[33] Tristan Gaudiaut, *"Russie : la popularité de Poutine en hausse depuis l'invasion de Ukraine "*, en.statista.com, April 5, 2022

In the eyes of the West, Vladimir Putin embodies evil, the one who provoked everything and who went so far as to brandish the nuclear threat. Although he denies it, he is the aggressor. He is the one who ordered his armies to intervene in Ukraine, for security purposes, although he quickly felt like attacking larger territories than those defended by the separatist troops. The facts do not speak in its favour. However, the origins of this military operation have a provocative character that is not unique to Russia. Within the Western alliance, the case of the annexation of Crimea has never been digested. In Russia, the tone is different. What is perceived as an annexation on the one hand and presented as a desire of the Crimeans to leave the Ukrainian fold and become part of Russia. The referendum held in 2014 is described as a farce in the West, while Moscow presents it as an expression of the people's attachment to Russia. In general, the West sees Russia as the villain and vice versa. As far as the conflict in Ukraine is concerned, we would probably be wrong to attribute all the blame to Russia. The West has a share of responsibility. There are wrongs on both sides.

With the arrival of Vladimir Putin to power, it was written that Russia would hope to regain a place of choice on the international political scene. Although he was propelled to power thanks to Boris Yeltsin, he did not want his country to simply approve of the will of the West, led by the United States. Russia had to assert itself. Strengthened by an economic revival linked to the increase in the exchange prices of hydrocarbons, it gradually managed to become a key player in international relations and to show its hostility to the West. In the eyes of Vladimir Putin, the great rival was none other than the United States. As for the European Union (EU), he reproached it for following the decisions of the American big brother. The master of the Kremlin has always considered that the end of the USSR was a huge geopolitical catastrophe. He has systematically shown distance and distrust towards the West, as in the heyday of the Cold War. There was no lack of reasons to strain diplomatic relations. Between the spying scandals, poisonings, and other newsworthy events, one could almost forget President Putin's animosity towards NATO. On this point, he had a very clear opinion on the question: it was unbearable for him to imagine that the Atlantic alliance could extend to his borders. In other words, he could not imagine Ukraine joining the organization. The same was true for Georgia. All Western support for Kiev and Tbilisi regarding possible EU or NATO membership was seen in Moscow as a provocation. In August 2008, in the run-up to the Summer Olympics, a war broke out between Russia and Georgia over the breakaway region of South Ossetia. This conflict extended to Abkhazia. At the time, the President of the Russian Federation was Dmitry Medvedev and Vladimir Putin was in charge of the government. The events in Georgia are eerily reminiscent of those in Ukraine in 2014 and 2022.

In sum, it is certain that the wars involving Russia and former Soviet republics are not just a warning. They are the result of deep disagreements between the Western world and Moscow. Russia takes action when it believes that Western "provocation" goes too far. Similarly, conflicts have systematically erupted when Ukraine and Georgia were presided over by pro-European and pro-NATO rulers. On the Western side, if the verbal support given to Kiev and Tbilisi has never failed to make Moscow react, the conflicts have always been approached with a certain distancing. By distancing, one must understand several parameters. Firstly, there have been verbal statements suggesting that Georgia and Ukraine could one day join the EU and / or NATO. Second, the West has almost always displayed a form of distancing itself from Ukraine and Georgia, despite verbal support, by stating that the issues of EU and / or NATO membership for these two countries are not topical. In other words, it is a way of not wanting to declare war on Russia. As for the wars between Russia and these countries, they have never had NATO reinforcements. Third, as we are seeing in the current conflict, while NATO is providing logistical support and member states are providing funds to Ukraine, President Biden has been very clear in stating that armed intervention against Russia would only occur if Russia were to engage in hostilities on territory administered by a NATO member jurisdiction. In other words, it is up to Ukraine to defend itself against the Russian offensive, despite the financial and logistical support that would be invaluable for the armed struggle.

The same applies to the EU. When the President of the European Commission told Euronews on February 28 that Ukraine was wanted in the EU, President Zelensky immediately seized the opportunity to demand that his country join without delay. The reality is that an EU membership for Ukraine is not on the agenda in Brussels. The EU and NATO are very cautious in their support for Ukraine and Georgia because of the risk of escalating tensions with Russia that any statement or action may bring. Does this mean that the Western world fears Moscow and is afraid to engage in a war with uncertain consequences? Certainly, NATO does not want an armed conflict with Russia. If Russia does not hesitate to intervene militarily, the Atlantic alliance considers armed intervention only as a last resort. Clearly, Russia and the Western world have a tumultuous relationship that has gone crescendo in intensity since the mid-2000s. Three wars have been launched since then: a first one in Georgia and two others in Ukraine. Faced with the military threat, the West favours another approach to retaliation: economic sanctions. On the other hand, the war taking place on the doorstep of several EU jurisdictions is a stark reminder of the need to be more prepared for an armed conflict. As a result, several governments have announced their intention to rapidly and significantly increase their national defense budgets.

We noticed that there is little mention of the Minsk and Minsk II Agreements concluded in 2014 and 2015, which aimed to establish an immediate ceasefire. While the first was never respected, the second was about constitutional reforms, the release and exchange of prisoners on both sides or the withdrawal of heavy weaponry. It is important to note that Ukraine initially did not want this agreement, which was led by Germany and France. However, since it had no peace agreement with Russia, it wanted to put an end to hostilities. There is no need to enter into legal debates about the validity of these multiparty agreements. The agreement covered thirteen points, but several were violated. In fact, the fighting in the Donbass region never stopped. Although Russia strongly denied sending troops and failing to comply with the Minsk II agreement, Russian hybrid forces continued military operations there. The West accused Moscow of sending fighters operating in civilian clothes. Similarly, point 11 refers to the Donetsk and Lugansk regions, which are referred to by the acronym ORDLO. The latter was never explicitly defined, while reference was made to a "special status". The agreement provided for amendments to the Ukrainian constitution, but these were never made. Other points of contention mean that the Minsk II Agreement has never been fully respected. We are thinking of the free elections that were supposed to be held in the Donbass and that could not be held because of the war and the fact that Ukraine does not control its border. Similarly, the Russians and Ukrainians do not agree on the terms of the amnesty negotiated on behalf of the ORDLO fighters. Russia wanted the amnesty to be granted before free elections in the

Donbass and before Ukraine regained control of the border. On the Kiev side, the amnesty was to be granted after these events.

In summary, several conditions of the Minsk II Agreement have never been implemented by either Russia or Ukraine. We will not enter into the debate of who is right or wrong; that is not the purpose of this reflection. What we do know is that there are facts that have certainly fuelled bitterness, resentment or anger in Kiev and Moscow, a state of tension that has never ceased to grow while both sides have blamed each other for not wanting to engage in a genuine peace process by transgressing the conditions agreed upon in Minsk II. Once again, none of this legitimizes a military operation that is in reality a declaration of war. However, we understand more that there are many reasons for tension, some from Russia, some from Ukraine and some from the Western alliance. Misunderstandings and initiatives deliberately put in place to provoke the ire of the opposing camp have contributed to this escalation of tensions that led to the irreparable: war.

We ask ourselves the age-old question: was the war avoidable? Was it possible to convince Russia not to intervene militarily? The French head of state Emmanuel Macron has spared no effort in trying to make diplomacy triumph. A month and a half after the outbreak of hostilities, several European governments are criticizing the fact that he is striving to give priority to diplomacy, while his detractors are arguing that one does not negotiate with a dictator... Let's give him credit: he has ventured where no one else has ventured. He tried. He went to Moscow to talk to Vladimir Putin. He has maintained a regular dialogue with Putin to try to avoid the dramatic outcome that we know. In view of everything that is reported by the media, the gap between Ukrainian and Russian demands seems immense, which tends to suggest that the war is likely to be prolonged. However, Russia is encountering difficulties that it had not anticipated. At the beginning of April, it abandoned part of the country to concentrate on the eastern regions. It is also rumoured that Moscow is preparing a major offensive there. As they left the Kiev region in particular, unbearable images made the media headlines: those of lifeless bodies in streets devastated by the fighting, too many civilian victims who were no doubt hoping for a peaceful resolution to the crisis.

GLOSSARY OF ABBREVIATIONS

AFP: Agence France-Presse (French international news agency)
AQIM: Al-Qaeda in the Islamic Maghreb
CIA: Central Intelligence Agency
CO2: Carbon dioxide
DoJ: Department of Justice
ECOWAS: Economic Community of West African States
ESG: Environment, Social and Governance
EU: European Union
FBI: Federal Bureau of Investigation
GAFA: Google Amazon Facebook Apple
GAFAM: Google Amazon Facebook Apple Microsoft
GHG: Greenhouse gases
IEA: International Energy Agency
INSEE: National Institute of Statistics and Economic Studies (French institute of statistics)
IPCC: Intergovernmental Panel on Climate Change
KYC: Know Your Client
LNG: Liquefied Natural Gas
LPG: Liquefied Petroleum Gas
NATO: North Atlantic Treaty Organization
NFT: Non-Fungible Tokens
NPT: Non-Proliferation Treaty
NRA: National Rifle Association
OBOR: One Belt, One Road
OPEC: Organization of the Petroleum Exporting Countries
PDVSA: Petróleos de Venezuela, SA
SCO: Shanghai Cooperation Organization
SME: Small and Medium Enterprises
TOE: Tons of Oil Equivalent
UN: United Nations
USSR: Union of Soviet Socialist Republics
WHO: World Health Organization
WTI: West Texas Intermediate
WTO: World Trade Organization

www.ingramcontent.com/pod-product-compliance
Lightning Source LLC
Chambersburg PA
CBHW070518160726
48003CB00004B/1616